Resilience and the Wandering Subject

Edited by

Supriya Daniel
IIT Bombay

Anu Kuriakose
NIT, Trichy

Series in Literary Studies

VERNON PRESS

In the Americas:
Vernon Press
1000 N West Street, Suite 1200,
Wilmington, Delaware 19801
United States

In the rest of the world:
Vernon Press
C/Sancti Espiritu 17,
Malaga, 29006
Spain

Series in Literary Studies

Library of Congress Control Number: 2024938414

ISBN: 979-8-8819-0122-6

Also available: 979-8-8819-0035-9 [Hardback]; 979-8-8819-0078-6 [PDF, E-Book]

Cover design by Vernon Press. Image by Anirban Bose.

Contents

Introduction

Supriya Daniel

IIT Bombay

> Finally, all these present struggles revolve around the question, Who are we? (Foucault 781)

Any investigation into "Who are we?" struggles to formulate an answer. This book "participates" (Derrida 65) in the quest to comprehend the essence of human beings from the two strands—"struggle" and "who"—which has been transliterated into resilience and subject/self/identity in the chapters that follow.[1] Resilience or "positive adaptation despite adversity" (Fleming and Ledogar 2) is captured as one of the forces that nudge the im/mobility of the subject and plays a pivotal part in the formation of identity.[2]

The formulation of the concept of the wandering subject that is reflected in this book emerges from my doctoral thesis, where the intention was to particularly analyse the ever-evolving and forming subject in contemporary novels from Africa. The context of extrapolating this concept of the subject was that the overriding Western thought, as criticized by Achille Mbebme, seems to depend on binaries that consequently give prominence to one as opposed to the other (2). So, either the self is markedly different and superior to the other, or the human is essentially rational and, therefore, not an animal. What happens when one does not inhabit the space of the subject as conceived by Western Enlightenment? How does one conceive what the human is when "the definition of what and who human was based on exclusion, so that the slave, the barbarian and the foreigner were ... figures of an animal in human form" (qtd. in Roos 67).[3]

---

[1] Jacques Derrida uses "participates" in the context of genres," Every text participates in one or several genres" (65), in the sense that the text does not commit to one particular genre. Similarly, the concepts discussed in the book, while examines concepts of subject/self/identity, does not claim to belong to one absolute strand of thought not claim to carve a unique pathway, but explore a different paradigm to understand these fluid concepts.

[2] S.S Luthar's definition of resilience from other definitions of resilience has been used here since this resonates with the idea of resilience in the book. Nevertheless, the introduction will glance upon the variations formations of resilience in the latter part.

[3] Daniel, Supriya. "Conjuring the ghostly storytelling space and subject in select novels from Africa."

Nevertheless, "'The Subject' is an elusive subject" (Strozier 10) even within the Western thought. While tracing the historical construction of "subject", Robert Strozier delineates the Subject from the already formed, a priori Subject of Aristotle and Kant to Foucault's discursive subject where power and knowledge network of discourses produces the subject (11).[4] Arguably, Foucauldian thought catapulted an upheaval in the discussion of "who are we?" that spilt into the discourses of identities and the usual markers of it as gender, race or nation.[5] One could perhaps even navigate to posthumanism which has compelled new conceptions of the human. However, critics like Sylvia Wynter and Charles W Mills call for a new humanism influenced by Franz Fanon's humanism.[6] They critique posthumanism as an alibi for further denial of humanity to the people who were never considered humans (Shu-mei 30).

In this context, it would be beneficial for the very formation of the subject discourse to garner voices from around the world to comprehend the nuances of the concept of the subject.

The aim of this compilation is to interject at this point of the discussion and offer the concept of wandering subject as one of the perspectives that allow an inclusion of a spectrum of voices and experiences and a modality to express the concept of subject in not fixed modes of thought processes.

The term "wandering subject", itself in the thesis and eventually in this book, is borrowed from Achille Mbembe's "Life, Sovereignty, and Terror in the Fiction of Amos Tutuola". His analysis of the beings in the Nigerian author Amos Tutuola's works reveals that:

> there is no body except in and through movement. That is why there is no subject but a wandering one. The wandering subject moves from one place to another. Journey as such does not need a precise destination: the wanderer can go about as he pleases. (17)

---

[4] Another compilation on the matter of subject that can aid this discussion is "Who Comes After Subject?" where Gerard Granel examines the different coordinates from which the (Western) subject has been understood. As an expansion of the notion of subject, he suggests that one who comes after the subject would be the one who has not been allowed to emerge as subjects "otherwise than as a people of production" (156), which is the existing mode of formation of the subject.

[5] The primary thoughts being of Judith Butler or the postcolonial discourses (refer Daniel, Supriya."Foucault and Postcolonialism: An African Perspective" in the journal *Critical Space*)

[6] In *Wretched of the Earth*, Fanon advocates his brand of humanism, which is multi-layered drawing from Western and African traditions. He argues, "if we want humanity to take one step forward, if we want to take it to another level than the one where Europe has placed it, then we must innovate, we must be pioneers" (238).

The subject that is in constant movement is also a "subject *au travail*, in the making" (16). The movement is not just the journey without a destination but also the constant change in form and content of the wandering subject.[7] Deployment of existence for this ever-changing subject can occur only when the subject leans "upon a reservoir of memories and images that are never fixed definitively" (23). The unstable and ever-changing "entity" or the wandering subject must "allow himself [sic] to be carried away by the flux of time and accidents" (23). The subjects produce themselves in the "chain of effects" that do not occur as was foreseen. It is in this flux that the subject invents "himself," thus negating any sovereignty to the subject.[8]

This book expands this concept of wandering subjects to understand myriad ways of the ever-evolving subject. The spirit of the concept, as elucidated in each chapter, ruminates about the other tangents through which we can comprehend the ever "elusive subject" (Strozier 10) that is in continual formation through struggle that exhibits resilience. Each chapter serves to exhume the concept of the wandering subject in its various nuances, situating the subject in several spaces and times, with emphasis on how acts of resilience are integral to the subject formation. The struggle emanates from the quest of "who we are?" as Foucault seems to suggest, and one could argue that "who we are" emerges from the struggle that one overcomes and in the process of resilience.

In the first chapter, "Women Walking the City: Analysing the Wandering Subject in Amrita Mahale's *Milk Teeth*", Namrata Nirmal and Merin Simi Raj elucidate the role of a woman as the flaneur in the city and devices the city through the wanderings of the woman. The wandering in this chapter is the physical mobility and the lack of it through the city, which is dominated by the male gaze. The wandering subject, then, becomes a mode of negotiation through the patriarchal, postcolonial urban space to find a footing, through resilient overtures, for the ones who have been excluded from these spaces.

The wandering subject's intertwining between the space of wandering is continued in the second chapter, "Home(in)g the Hostland: Provincializing Metropolitan Cities of Refuge in Sethu's *The Saga of Muziris*". The urban space is again invoked but as a refuge for a community. While both the chapters articulate from a postcolonial urban space, this chapter examines this space as a shelter for the migrating Jewish community. The wanderings of the displaced

---

[7] Mbembe quotes passages from Tutuola's novels to show the dismembered bodies and how they get mixed up and entangled.

[8] Refer Supriya Daniel's "Conjuring the ghostly storytelling space and subject in select novels from Africa."

community, as they continue in the city, configure their self and identity in the act of resilience and hope generated in the city that serves as their home.

The quest for home emerges in the wanderings of the protagonist in Le Guin's novel to overcome trauma and find home. In the third chapter, "In Search of a Home: A Queer Hero's Quest to Belong", Aleena Achamma Paul argues that the protagonist's mobility, spurred by trauma and the need for belongingness, serves to inspect the act of resilience or heroism leads to the discovery of self of the wandering subject. The chapter draws parallels to historical events and other science fiction to re-affirm that the wandering subject does not just emerge in certain fictional works but is a concept that can be used as a framework to elucidate subject formation.

Continuing with the motif of a journey in a hostile environment from the previous chapter, the fourth chapter, "Carrying the Fire: *The Road* and Rituals of Resilience in a Dead World", extrapolates the idea of the constant movement of the wandering subject without a destination. The road they travel evokes a sense of the journey itself being the destination. The mobility of the subject is encumbered with the task of upholding optimism in the face of chaos and destruction. The resilience and insistence on being the "good guys" even when the odds are compiled against the subject become the only constant in the wanderings.

Moving on from speculative and dystopian worlds to a postcolonial one, the fifth chapter, "'Masi': The Wandering Subject in "Wake Up Call" in *Barbed Wire Fence* (2015)", positions the unreliable narrator, Masi, to explore the concept of identity from a marginalized space. The setting and the character of the story selected to illustrate the concept of wandering subject provide ample scope to comprehend the complexity of the wandering subject that arises from "ghostly" figures like Masi who are in spaces where they are considered as non-entities struggling to find citizenship in a nation where they are in the periphery and lost in the process of documentation.

Ijeoma Odoh, in the next chapter, "Construction of Maternal/Womb Space and Her-story in Andrea Levy's *Small Island*", through a reappropriation of Deleuze and Guattari's concept of the rhizome, excavates the concept of the wandering subject through the women who are forced to migrate—through the routes and connections they undertake to re-form their identities. The identity formation seeps beyond the usual compartmentalization of race, gender, class and nation to foster new connections and render voice to the voiceless in their resilient search for change through migration.

The penultimate chapter, "Resilience as a Form of Contestation in the Poetry of John Clare", breaks away from the journeys of the subject within the text to the subject producing the text. Anindita Chatterjee chronicles the life and work of the poet John Clare as a resilient voice who defied any sense of fixed identities. His poems reflective of his marginalised status, pours the angst of the lack of comprehension of his 'true' self. Perhaps the subject within the text and without, are mirror images of the same self.

The last chapter, "*Mise en Abîme*: A Strategy that Highlights a Wandering, Fluid Subjectivity in Abdallah Laroui's novel *Awrāq: Sīrat Idrīs al-dhihniyyah*", delves into the novel to discover means of deciphering and portraying the wandering subject. The narrative device of *mise en abîme* allows us to further dissect the concept of the wandering subject's lack of a fixed definition, as embedded in this concept is the idea of mobility. This traversing is not just through physical spaces but through self and time. The subject, never being constant and always evolving, renders marking its boundaries an impossible and unnecessary task. Subsequently, providing further insights to elucidate the wandering subject.

Works Cited

Daniel, Supriya."Foucault and Postcolonialism: An African Perspective." *Critical Space*, vol. 9, no.2, 2021.

Derrida, Jacques. "The Law of Genre." Trans. Avital Ronell. *Critical Inquiry* vol.7, no.1,1980, pp. 55.

Foucault, Michel. "The Subject and Power". *Critical Inquiry* vol. 8, no. 4,1982, pp. 777-795.

Fleming, John, and Robert J Ledogar. "Resilience, an Evolving Concept: A Review of Literature Relevant to Aboriginal Research." *Pimatisiwin* vol. 6, no.2, 2008, pp.7-23.

Fanon, Franz. *The Wretched of the Earth*. Presence Africaine, 1963.

Granel, Gerard. "Who Comes after the Subject." Eds. Cadava, Eduardo, Peter Connor, and Jean-Luc Nancy. *Who Comes after the Subject?* New York: Routledge, 1991. 148-57.

Mbembe, Achille. "Life, Sovereignty, and Terror in the Fiction of Amos Tutuola." *Research in African Literatures* vol.34, no.4, 2003, pp. 1-26.

Roos, Henriette. "'The War of the Worlds:' Relocating the Boundaries Between the Human and the Non-Human." *Journal of Literary Studies* vol.27, no.4, 2011. pp. 50-70.

Shih, Shu-mei. "Is the Post- in Postsocialism the Post- in Posthumanism?". *Social Text* vol.30, no.1,2012, pp.27-50.

Strozier, Robert M. *Foucault, Subjectivity, and Identity: Historical Constructions of Subject*. Wayne State University Press, 2002.

Chapter 1

Women Walking the City: Analysing the Wandering Subject in Amrita Mahale's *Milk Teeth*

Namrata Nirmal

IIT Madras, India

Merin Simi Raj

IIT Madras, India

Abstract

Urban spaces, mostly perceived as male preserves, have traditionally been narrated in orientation to male subjectivity. From the earliest discussions in Western scholarship, the street is considered to be the default location of the everyday and the *flâneur* its hero. Through an outline of the history of this figure and its various theoretical renderings, this article proposes an intervention in the Indian context by tracing how the female urban dweller has been conceived over the years in diverse narrative spaces. In this context, the article argues, viewing the urban walker as a wandering subject allows for a renewed understanding of gender and the city in literature. The separation of the public and private spheres and the consequent sexual division of society, is a crucial moment in this chequered history. Yet, women find ways to negotiate this boundary. This process of negotiation and transgression needs to be critically examined, particularly about how participation in the labour force affords them mobility. Thus, the city in women's writing emerges as a site of contestation between the public and the private, freedom and confinement, access and risk. The article explores the literary representation of women's experience of the city, with a focus on Indian English fiction. Using the novel *Milk Teeth* (2018) by Amrita Mahale as a narrative point of entry, the paper examines the relationship between urban space and the wandering subject. Drawing on the frameworks of spatiality and female experience, this article underlines the transformative potential of urban writing, which deserves closer and more incisive critical attention from interdisciplinary perspectives.

Keywords: Female Experience, Flâneur, Urban Space, Urban Walking, Wandering Subject

***

I

This study seeks to unpack how urban spaces have been configured and calibrated in postcolonial narratives through an incisive engagement with select texts and contexts. Accordingly, it tries to situate the figure of the flâneur, with flânerie being considered as a practice of observing everyday city life but also as a tool significant to the writing process. Despite its Eurocentric origin, over the years, the flâneur has been reimagined in diverse contexts and periods. This article delineates the history of this figure and its various theoretical renderings, particularly in the postcolonial context, through the critical reading of a contemporary representative text. Subsequently, it proposes an intervention in the Indian context by tracing how the female urban dweller has been conceived over the years in diverse narrative spaces. Such an analysis of the interplay of gender and the city in literature is aided by viewing the urban walker as a wandering subject. The public life of women, or the lack thereof, has long been regulated by the notion of respectability. The prevalence of the separate spheres ideology and the consequent sexual division of society is a crucial moment in this chequered history. Yet, women find ways to negotiate this boundary. This process of negotiation and transgression needs to be critically examined, particularly about how participation in the labour force affords them mobility. Thus, the city in women's writing emerges as a site of contestation between the public and the private, freedom and confinement, access and risk.

This article explores the literary representation of women's experience of the city, with a focus on Indian English fiction. Being a work of imagination, fiction is useful in studying how urban women have been thought of and written about over the years. The city was always envisaged as a masculine space across nations and cultures; however, one can identify several Western/European texts where the possibility of women navigating urban spaces was explored in varying degrees. This is a literary and cultural trend which may be traced back to texts as early as Emile Zola's *The Ladies' Paradise* where the modern woman was situated within an emergent capitalist space, namely, the department store. Unlike the Western imaginary, postcolonial Indian writing in English had largely narrativised urban women within domestic spaces, as evinced in the novels of Kamala Markandeya, Anita Desai, Nayantara Sahgal, Ruth Prawer

Jhabvala and the likes who dominated Indian fiction in English through the 1970s and 1980s (Mehrotra 227–230). However, at the same time, the metropolitan cities that emerged as extensions of colonial modernity even before Independence also had hamlets where the imaginative and literal wanderings of women were possible, though only marginally. This liminal anxiety was perhaps captured in novels of the early twentieth century, such as *Sultana's Dream* (1905) by Rokeya Sakhawat Hossein, where the protagonist finds herself rather oddly placed when she ventures to wander the streets like a man. Using the novel *Milk Teeth* (2018) by Amrita Mahale as a narrative point of entry, this article examines the relation between urban space and the wandering subject, thereby relocating female subjectivity. The novel, which is a telling departure from the dominant narrative trends which relegated women to the domestic, follows two childhood friends, Ira Kamat and Kartik Kini, who grew up in the same apartment building in Matunga, Mumbai. After years of estrangement, they reconnect as adults on the terrace of Asha Nivas while its residents decide the fate of the establishment— to accept the offer of redevelopment or not. Throughout the novel, the relationship between the protagonists morphs in tandem with the unfolding contestations over their building. Ira and Kartik rekindle their friendship, and then form a surprising marital alliance, which later meets a swift end at the hint of infidelity. The character of Ira, a civic beat journalist, is of particular interest. She is a peripatetic figure, constantly flitting between the public and the private, work and home, deviance and respectability. The novel is set in the 1990s. The discourse of this decade focused overwhelmingly on the impact of liberalisation and globalisation, which were most evident in the economic, social, political and cultural landscape of Bombay/Mumbai. Posited as a global city, it was— and continues to be—home to the wealthiest individuals in the country. Its well-off residents participated in the growth of consumer culture, largely derived from the West, that dictated their behaviour, dressing sense, food choices, and leisure activities. The middle-class, beneficiaries in this new economy, aspired towards higher standards of urban living. Talks of development pervaded conversations across the city. At the same time, the city's entry into the global economic network coincided with the rise of religious fundamentalism. The communal riots of this decade and the ensuing violence culminated in the changing of the city's name from Bombay to Mumbai in 1995 (Kamdar 75–77). Many scholars have remarked that this moment signified the death of cosmopolitanism in the city. Much of the literature on Mumbai has since focused on the name change as a political event, reading it as a change in the identity of the city from secular to intolerant, cosmopolitan to nativist. *Milk Teeth* also traces this transition.

II

The relationship between the everyday and the city has long fascinated urban scholars. The modern city, as a way of life distinct from the rural, began to be articulated in the early nineteenth century. This was accompanied by an interest in everyday life, or, conversely, the conditions of urban life were such that it produced the everyday as an object of interest. Industrialisation played a substantial role in alienating urban residents. As the city was comprised of isolated individuals who did not know each other, the chance encounter in the street was considered as definitive of the urban experience (Bown 75–78).

French philosopher Henri Lefebvre's writing on cities is seminal to the scholarship on the everyday as he drew attention to the representation of space from above—for instance, by an urban development authority through planning and mapping exercises—and how the everyday may deviate from this representation. He raised questions of who owns the city, who has a right to it, and who is excluded from its conceptualisation (Tambling 3). Similarly, Michel de Certeau highlighted the city as a site of contestation. One view of the city, which he terms the "concept-city", is held by the voyeur who looks at the city from above, keeping a distance in order to rationalise it to make it legible. This view is held by the urbanist, the city planner, or the cartographer. The other view is that of the urban walker, "the ordinary practitioners of the city", who navigate the bustle of streets that is left out of the gaze of the voyeur. Certeau proposed walking as a spatial practice that transgresses the map of the concept of city and, thus, of panoptic power. Mobility is key to his proposition—a map may be able to trace the paths taken by city dwellers, but it cannot capture the act of passing by (de Certeau 110–115).

Apart from its radical possibilities, the continued interest in the everyday is also due to its elusive nature. It escapes definition and resists theorisation. How, then, can one capture the everyday? Ben Highmore suggests that art and literature serve as mediums through which the everyday finds articulation (3). The spatial turn of the 2000s in literary studies suggests that this relationship between the city and literature has not gone unnoticed. Lefebvre and de Certeau's work, although rooted in the European context, provide clues to reading the postcolonial city. Official conceptions of the city, as promoted by panoptic (colonial) power, make invisible certain histories and experiences of the marginalised (Herbert 202–203). As Frantz Fanon pointed out, the colony was essential to urbanising the West to constructing its narrative of progress. Modernity was always elsewhere but certainly not to be found in the colonial city (58). This historical and political context is important to making sense of the postcolonial city. Recent scholarship on the subject highlights three approaches in this regard: first, a critique of the neo-colonial image of cities in the global South as overpopulated and underdeveloped; second, an interrogation of the

Western concepts of modernity and development in the context of urbanisation; and third, a recognition of the impact of these concepts on urban imaginaries and aspirations in the global South (Sandten and Bauer xiv).

With the spatial turn, the notion of the city as palimpsest found relevance in postcolonial literature. These texts experiment with narrative space, using techniques such as non-linear storytelling and multiple points of view in order to reflect the dizzying experience of the urban in new and emerging metropolises. They take into account the evolving position of these cities in the global economic network. They present the city as layered, with overlapping and competing histories, identities, and memories. In this manner, postcolonial literature complicates the ideas of citizenship and belonging in urban spaces (Sandten and Bauer xv).

What is missing from this discourse is the crucial question of gender. If walking the streets is one way to claim ownership of the city, women are already excluded from the protest. The anonymity that this act requires is rarely available to women. The separation of the workplace from the home further cemented the sexual division of nineteenth-century society. The dominant ideology was that women's rightful place was in the domestic realm. No respectable woman would wander the streets alone (Wolff 37). Similarly, women remain invisible in every conception of the postcolonial city. While the possibility of a postcolonial flâneur has been explored, not much has been written about the public life of women (Williams, 1997). Scholarship on urban spaces in Indian literature tends to focus on portraying the character of specific cities and the historical moments that altered their fabric. Most engagements with gender emphasise the domestic, interior lives of women.

The distinction between the public and the private reappears here. The demand for a sovereign nation-state brought with it the need to establish an alliance, however uneasy, between modernity and tradition. In India, nationalists separated the concerns of the two into the domains of the material and the spiritual, respectively. In the external matters of politics, statecraft, science, and technology, Indians must learn and adapt European models—which were conceded to be superior. However, the sacred matters of culture and religion must not suffer from any such foreign influences. Thus, the dichotomy of the outside and the inside, the world and the home, was imbibed with nationalist meaning. Additionally, the home being the province of the woman dictated her role as the guardian of native culture. Patriarchal gender roles were further crystallised due to this ideology (Chatterjee 116–121). Consequently,

> the woman in the city, the archetypal new woman, is both a sign of modernity and its radical other. She represents the moral dangers of modern life as embodied in the figure of the prostitute, or the potential

or a partially realised, decolonised Indian subjectivity in the figure of the modern housewife. (Varma 126)

Thus, the urban woman was a problem for the nationalist project because she adhered neither to the mould of the authentic postcolonial subject rooted in tradition nor that of the individualistic Western subject tainted by feminist ideals.

However, feminist critics have made attempts to challenge existent writing on cities, drawing attention to the overwhelmingly male perspective of these narratives. The late twentieth century marked a renewed interest in the figure of the flâneur. Popularised by Walter Benjamin, the flâneur is a detached observer of urban society who wanders through the streets as everyday life unfolds around him. For Benjamin, modernity was to be found in the sensory experiences and chance encounters of the city, and the flânerie was central to writing about it (Moore 59). Feminist scholars speculated the possibility of a female flâneur—or a *flâneuse*. Rachel Bowlby chronicled the role of the department store in providing women access to the city, likening the consumer to the flâneur, both casting their fetishizing gaze on the urban spectacle (Parsons 47–50). Elizabeth Wilson, while recognising that the city is discriminative by design, refused to victimise their position, explaining her stance as "a matter of emphasis whether one insists on the dangers or the opportunities for women in cities" (83). Deborah Parsons took recourse to literature, exploring women's writing in London and Paris from 1880 to 1940, searching for articulations of the flâneuse (39–42). More recently, Lauren Elkin has looked at women walking the various cities she herself has inhabited, covering forms as diverse as fiction, journalism, to photography. For instance, she suggests that the reporter is a contemporary manipulation of the flâneur in that journalism is more of an intentional activity, with an endpoint in mind—i.e., covering and disseminating the news—contradictory to the aimless walking that was characteristic of flânerie in its earlier understanding (Elkin 233). Rashmi Varma has deployed the figure of "unhomely women" who skirt between the public and the private, bound to neither sphere. This term aims to subvert the dominant assumption that the presence of women in the city, outside their purported domain, is "unhomely". This is yet another response to the flâneur, as Varma notes that "the figure of 'unhomely women' performs an ironic gendered re-citation of the quintessential 'unhomely' figure of modernist urbanism that was the flâneur" (Varma 26).

Such redefinitions of the flâneur—its gendered appropriations, its contemporary manipulations—attest to the liberating potential of the city. Moreover, such an endeavour problematises the home as a safe haven and, conversely, the street as dangerous. This line of thought is a feature of cultural ethnography as well. Shilpa Phadke's work on gender and the politics of space in Mumbai disrupts the public/private, danger/safety dichotomy by drawing attention to the fact that women are more likely to be harassed by someone they know, typically a family member. The construction of this dichotomy hides the reality of domestic violence. Moreover, it denies women free and fair access to public space—a right, she argues, of all urban citizens. In fact, their very presence in the street is questioned, particularly if not for the justifiable reason of work. Going out in search of pleasure, to simply have fun, is a tricky task for women even today and involves a ridiculous amount of subterfuge and strategy. In order to reclaim the city, then, women must engage in the radical act of loitering: hanging around in public without purpose—a suggestion strikingly similar to flânerie but proposed in an entirely different social, political, and geographical context (Phadke 2–4).

In this context, perceiving the female urban walker as a wandering subject facilitates a renewed understanding of gender and the city in literature. The historian Achille Mbembe defines the wandering subject in relation to mobility. "The body is made first and foremost to move, to walk, which is why every subject is a wandering subject" (144). However, not every subject has equal access and opportunity to wander the city. As Natalie Collie asks, "What difference … do different bodies make to these [spatial] practices, and to the urban spaces, stories, and subjectivities that they articulate?" (4). Taking mobility as central to female subject formation, understood in relation to urban space, opens up the discussion of agency, freedom, access, and risk in the city. This brings the literature review to a full circle.

III

In the novel *Milk Teeth*, the protagonist Ira's journalistic practice can be read as a manipulation of flânerie. As a reporter on the civic beat, her occupation takes her all over Mumbai. She talks to people from different walks of life—politicians, middlemen, citizens—to scope for a story. The first time that readers witness her on the job, she is inspecting stormwater drains in the suburbs with the help of a former municipal civil engineer. With the monsoon season soon upon them, the shoddy work of contractors was up for scrutiny. She finds that most of the *nullahs* (drains) had not been cleaned nor dredged, leaving the city woefully unprepared for the coming onslaught of the rains. Ira's profession has none of the glamour that flânerie holds. She spends the morning weaving through jam-packed traffic, looking at sludge-filled drains. Then, there is the monotony. The story remained the same every year: a *jhol* (scam) was uncovered, fingers were pointed, corruption was condemned—and then the city would flood once again.

At times it felt like there was nothing new left to say about Mumbai. More often than not, work had become one routine story braided into another.... The big stories appeared to be in hiding. The elusive aha moment skulked around her, invisible and biding. In its place there were only false starts and dead ends. All thunder and no rain. (Mahale 46)

Even so, Mumbai surprises her in the midst of this monotony. On her way back home, she witnesses a fight in the ladies' compartment of the local train, with one woman cursing in the most colourful, creative language. Moments like these, a part of the urban spectacle, remind Ira of how imaginative the inhabitants of her city can be (Ibid. 43–48).

Ira holds the city and her neighbourhood close to her heart. This is evident in her work as well. When her newspaper proposes a series to mark 50 years of Mumbai since Independence, she proposes that they include an article on Matunga. As the first suburb of the island city, planned in the aftermath of the plague, it was envisioned as an area with wide roads, open spaces, and parks. In the 1920s, it primarily attracted the middle-classes, and over the years, the so-called suburb was subsumed within the growing city. Ira suggests that they compare this vision of Matunga to the definition of development in the 1990s (Ibid 110–111). This suggestion is guided by her political stance as well as personal stake. Ira is critical of the burgeoning ambitions that Mumbai had come to symbolise. Their manifestation in the everyday life of the city is of particular interest to her. In the novel, she muses about how, in some ways, the lane that housed Asha Nivas, her apartment building, had stayed the same since her childhood. A peal of bells rang out periodically from the three temples in the locality. A strip of the road was occupied by the flower market. The trees overhead shaded the street as always. Yet, over the years, this scene had transformed in some conspicuous ways as well. Cars took up precious real estate on the roadside. A new bank appeared in the area. Old buildings were replaced by swanky condominiums with names that sounded out of place: Belle View, Santorini Towers, and Eiffel Enclave (Mahale 24–25).

As discussions on the redevelopment of Asha Nivas move forward, it appears as though the face of her neighbourhood and its very fabric will be transformed. She wonders, "What will happen to Matunga if it becomes a collection of tall buildings cramped next to each other?" (Ibid. 269). As her job brings her in contact with the poorest inhabitants of Mumbai, she is unable to see how the prevailing idea of development could be sustainable. Her fears are not unfounded, as political writing from the time declares that "Bombay's congestion makes it impossible for the rich to flee the poor" (qtd. in Varma 130). Ira is critical of this neo-colonial Western influence, which continues to dictate the trajectory of cities in India. Arguably, her reportage attempts to override the concept-city envisioned by the state. Questions about the right to the city and the claims made to its spaces emerge in her writing, even as her own people—family, neighbours, fellow middle-class residents—rage against any hint of welfarism.

Hence, Ira's journalistic practice—of both walking and writing—remains critically aware of the deep-seated inequalities that Mumbai exhibits despite her obvious attachment to the city.

Perhaps it would be useful to contrast this with other walks that the novel outlines. For instance, after Ira's first meeting with Kaiz, an architecture student who tags along on her routine covering of a corporation meeting, the two end up talking over tea. On the way to the bakery, he tells her stories of the numerous buildings they pass by, equipped as he is with historical knowledge of the city (Mahale 121–122). This is a feature of the innumerable walks they take together later. Since the time she has known him, but more so after his return from the United States—that is, after the communal riots and the name change to Mumbai—Kaiz is nostalgic for the Bombay of the past. For a city that was not truly his home—he had spent his childhood in Delhi—he worshipped it to the point of constructing some sense of belonging to it. Kaiz may be yearning for the past, but he has some of the markers of a nineteenth-century flâneur: a lack of necessity for employment and a tendency to romanticise the city. His aimless wandering, compared with Ira's purposeful walking, reveals the ways in which their gender and class positions shape their experience of the city as well as their outlook toward it. However, it must be noted that in the aftermath of the riots, Kaiz faces his own challenges in navigating the city as a Muslim man, and this is what causes him to leave for the US. Yet another example is that of Kartik, the other narrator of the novel. Readers are witnesses to the change in his relationship with Mumbai as he moves out of his parents' home (and then back) and rediscovers the city through his identity as a gay man. Kartik's Bombay made up of public toilets, chatrooms, and gay nights at a bar, is wildly different from the officious discourse of the city, invisible to those uninitiated to the codes of the LGBT community. There is scope for a study of how sexuality manifests in the built environment and the challenges in finding spaces where one will be accepted. Although further discussion of these challenges is beyond the scope of this article, these competing experiences of and relationships to Mumbai highlight its palimpsestic nature.

To circle back to the connection between journalism and walking as a spatial practice, one cannot ignore that for Ira, and for women in general, work is what legitimises their presence in the public eye. They are not always leisurely flâneurs taking in the city but also purposeful flâneuses, steadily walking towards their next destination. The feminist endeavour to go beyond Benjamin's definition, to invent the flâneuse, aims to make women visible in theoretical work on cities, to focus on the ways in which their interactions with the city are unique and different from that of men. Mahale's decision to write Ira as a civic beat journalist, as making sense of the city and her relationship to it, can be read as a deliberate choice to contribute to a literature that focalises the oft-overlooked female urban dweller.

IV

The dilemma of the female urban writer thus continues: how can she navigate the dichotomy of the public and the private? The two spheres are inextricably linked. Viewing their connection as complementary, rather than contradictory, will provide a more accurate understanding of women's experience in the contemporary metropolis—for the walk must ultimately lead to the flâneuse home. Varma's idea of "unhomely women" is useful in reading *Milk Teeth*. If the Indian woman is the carrier of tradition, relegated to the private domain, her appearance in public life is considered "unhomely". The figure of unhomely women negotiates between agency and structure, public and private, world and home, as they attempt to define themselves as urban citizens (Varma 21–26).

Ira does enjoy a great degree of freedom, owing to the financial independence that her job provides her as well as her occupation as a civic beat reporter. This freedom allows her to grieve in public when Kaiz breaks off their relationship. The heartbreak leads her out of the house and into the street. She walks every day; weeks and months are lost to this period of mourning, wherein movement is the only distraction from her pain. Mahale embeds Ira's emotions into the city's landscape, as everything is a reminder of what once was. For instance,

> she fears the yellow-and-black phone booths on the way. The letters STD ISO PCO beckon, they promise false hope. Tears come, like local trains, every couple of minutes. When she cries, people look, then look away; it's the code of this city, to look away from someone in private distress, a code as solid as 022. (Mahale 163)

It is possible to state that Ira, as a wandering subject, nearly achieves anonymity in the crowd. Briefly, she is both a spectacle and a spectator. At the same time, Ira does not escape the burden of negotiation. She is not a single woman living alone in the city; she must return to her family at the end of the day. While work legitimises her presence in the street, accessing public space for pleasure continues to be a task mired in strategy and deception. Her odd working hours are rightfully due to her being a journalist, but they provide a convenient cover to be outside the house for longer periods, especially at night. More daring are the lies about her outstation trips. In truth, these are excuses to stay over at boyfriends' places or go out of town with them. Ira's parents are not the extremely conservative kind; they are willing to permit her to marry a "friend" if she finds one, but any hint of sexual relations would be unacceptable (Ibid. 36–38). Towards the end of the novel, when Ira reconnects with Kaiz, she accompanies him to Alibaug, a nearby coastal town, for a party. In order to achieve this feat, she tells her parents and Kartik—now her fiancé—that it was a team retreat to celebrate the success of her newspaper's Independence Day series. While she has no qualms about lying to her parents, deceiving Kartik does not sit right with her; she comes clean to him afterwards (Ibid. 194). However, in the end, what leads to the breaking off of her engagement is not her freedom to roam around the city but the scandal of her dalliance with a Muslim man.

What does such negotiation imply about the place of women in the city? To constantly question their access to public space is to deny them this right as urban citizens. Conversely, constructing the home as a shelter from the dangerous street is to instil a false sense of security. Varma once again uses the figure of unhomely women to problematise the supposed safety of the private sphere, arguing that such a construction ignores the threat of domestic violence (Varma 27). In a similar vein, Phadke points out that the fear of sexual harassment in public at the hands of a stranger, although valid, is statistically less likely as compared to domestic violence perpetrated by a family member. Yet, women have to demonstrate purpose and manufacture safety in order to go out. Phadke proposes that in order to reclaim the city, women must be allowed the right to take risks. This can be achieved through loitering, simply hanging around in public without purpose. Acknowledging the long tradition of this activity and the vast literature of its gendered appropriation, Phadke is quick to urge that this is not a niche concern of privileged middle-class women but a movement about reclaiming public space for all citizens (Phadke 2–4). Read together, Varma and Phadke both attempt to define postcolonial feminist citizenship, what implications it has for society, and how women may strive for it.

V

Wandering holds radical potential in claiming the city—for women, as well as others on the margins of society. The epilogue to *Milk Teeth* emphasises the importance of striving for a more equitable world by depicting one evening in Ira's life. She interviews people in a public park about the increasing moral policing of young couples in one of the last remaining public spaces in the city. After wrapping up her work for the day, she stops by an Udupi restaurant, where she is a regular, for a quick bite. On the way home, she loiters around Asha Nivas, now covered in scaffolding as the redevelopment talks had finally worked out. Her family, however, had moved out early to save face after the broken engagement. She continues to note the changes in the built environment: a proposed flyover here and a new high-rise apartment there (Mahale 302–304). As always, Ira, as a wandering subject, is excessively fond of her city and yet maintains a critical distance from it. This is an inherent part of her journalistic practice, over which she ponders on this walk back home: "My work feels like a part of a long arc that bends toward an answer to that fundamental question: how should our society be?" (Ibid. 307). Mahale ends with this note on the transformative potential of urban writing—of not just Ira's work but perhaps her own fictional narrative as well.

This article has attempted to highlight this sense of being part of a larger (literary) tradition by reading *Milk Teeth* as a significant contemporary text in the long history of women's writing on cities. The postcolonial city has, above all else, been associated with chaos and flux—of people, architecture, identities, and ideologies. Wandering the city, then, emerges as a tool to navigate this chaos and encounter it up close. Lefebvre's thesis on the revolutionary potential of the everyday ties into de Certeau's proposal of walking as a spatial practice that subverts the rationalising gaze of the state. Together, they raise the question of who owns the city and, consequently, draw attention to who is excluded from it. This has specific implications for the postcolonial city, whose theorisation must include scrutiny of the neo-colonial influence of the so-called 'developed' global North on these spaces. The nature of the exclusion is, moreover, gendered as women are often erased from narratives of the urban. Recent work by scholars such as Varma and Phadke fills a significant gap in the literature on urban women in India. In sketching the contours of a feminist city, they use imagination as a tool to theorise the city in a positive light. Fiction further widens the scope of this discourse by speculating on the lives of urban women through the years: whether there was a female urban consciousness and whether they identified as rightful citizens of such a space. This does not imply that fiction ignores the challenges women encounter in traversing the urban landscape. Rather, it is a matter of emphasis: to look at the mobility women enjoy in the city and the ways in which they negotiate with the patriarchal elements in their lives to attain them. Ultimately, the city in women's writing emerges as a site of contestation between the public and the private, freedom and confinement, access and risk.

Works Cited

Bown, Alfie. "'How Did the Everyday Manage to Become So Interesting?'" *The Palgrave Handbook of Literature and the City*, edited by Jeremy Tambling, Palgrave Macmillan, 2016, pp. 75–87.

Chatterjee, Partha. *The Nation and its Fragments: Colonial and Postcolonial Histories*. Princeton University Press, 1993.

Collie, Natalie. "Walking in the City: Urban Space, Stories, and Gender." *Gender Forum: An Internet Journal for Gender Studies*, no. 42, 2013, pp. 1–7.

De Certeau, Michel. *The Practice of Everyday Life*. Translated by Steven Randall, University of California Press, 1984.

Elkin, Lauren. *Flaneuse: Women Walk the City in Paris, New York, Tokyo, Venice, and London*. Farrar, Straus and Giroux, 2016.

Fanon, Frantz. *The Wretched of the Earth*. Grove Atlantic, 2004.

Herbert, Caroline. "Postcolonial Cities." *The Cambridge Companion to the City in Literature*, edited by Kevin McNamara, Cambridge University Press, 2014, pp. 200–215.

Highmore, Ben. "Introduction: Questioning Everyday Life." *The Everyday Life Reader*, edited by Highmore, Routledge, 2002, pp. 1–34.

Kamdar, Mira. "Bombay/Mumbai: The Postmodern City." *World Policy Journal*, vol. 14, no. 2, 1997, pp. 75–88.

Mahale, Amrita. *Milk Teeth*. Context, 2019.

Mehrotra, Arvind Krishna. *An Illustrated History of Indian Literature in English*. Orient Blackswan, 2005.

Mbembe, Achilles. *Critique of Black Reason*. Duke University Press, 2017.

Parsons, Deborah L. *Streetwalking the Metropolis: Women, the City and Modernity*. Oxford University Press, 2000.

Phadke, Shilpa. "Defending Frivolous Fun: Feminist Acts of Claiming Public Spaces in South Asia." *South Asia: Journal of South Asian Studies*, vol. 43, no. 2, 2020, pp. 1–13.

Sandten, Cecile and Annika Bauer. "Re-inventing the Postcolonial (in the) Metropolis: An Introduction." *Re-inventing the Postcolonial (in the) Metropolis*, edited by Cecile Sandten and Annika Bauer, Brill, 2016, pp. xi–xxi.

Tambling, Jeremy. "Prologue: City-theory and Writing, in Paris and Chicago: Space, Gender, Ethnicity." *The Palgrave Handbook of Literature and the City*, edited by Jeremy Tambling, Palgrave Macmillan, 2016, pp. 1–22.

Varma, Rashmi. *The Postcolonial City and its Subjects: London, Nairobi, Bombay*. Routledge, 2012.

Williams, Adebayo. "The Postcolonial Flaneur and Other Fellow Travellers: Conceits for a Narrative of Redemption." *Third World Quarterly*, vol. 18, no. 5, 1997, pp. 821–841.

Wilson, Elizabeth. *The Contradictions of Culture: Cities, Culture, Women*. SAGE Publications, 2001.

Wolff, Janet. "The Invisible Flaneuse: Women and the Literature of Modernity." *Theory, Culture & Society* vol. 2, no. 37, 1985, pp. 37–46.

Chapter 2

Home(in)g the Hostland: Provincializing Metropolitan Cities of Refuge in Sethu's *The Saga of Muziris*

Jintu Alias

SRM University AP, India

Abstract

This chapter inspects the novel *The Saga of Muziris* by Sethu to examine the ways in which the space of Cochin provided a refugee-friendly environment for the Jewish community and fostered their well-being during their residency. The concept of the "wandering subject" and the relationship between wanderers and the spaces they occupy are pivotal to this analysis. The Jewish community, often associated with rootlessness and displacement, finds resonance as wanderers within this theoretical framework. Contrasting prevailing narratives, the novel facilitates unique perspectives on the Jewish experience, highlighting the hospitality and cultural autonomy that characterized Cochin. By provincializing the idea of cities of refuge and focusing on overlooked regional spaces, the article intends to underscore the pertinence of Cochin's unique history and geography, challenging conventional notions of metropolitan spatiality. Through an exploration of Sethu's novel, this study contributes to the broader project of reimagining literary geographies and widening our understanding of hostlands and exile. The article advocates for the recognition of local and provincial spaces as great examples of refuge spaces and highlights Cochin as a compelling example.

Keywords: wandering subjects, cities of refuge, region, provincialize, Cochin

***

Introduction

The act of wandering or migration has been an indispensable part of human history. There have been voluntary and involuntary migrations driven by the search for better economic, social, political and employment opportunities. Wandering Subject as a theoretical term was popularized by Achille Mbembe to indicate a person who "moves from one place to another" without a clear sense of destination or permanence (Mbembe and Mitsch 17). With no fixed sense of personality, these subjects are "carried away by the flux of time and accidents"(Mbembe and Mitsch 23). The concept of a wanderer got expanded and redefined when Georg Simmel combined the conflicting ideas of wandering and fixation to form the figure of a "potential wanderer", i.e, the stranger (Simmel 1). He argues that the stranger is a curious figure who is "fixed within a spatial group or within a group whose boundaries are similar to spatial boundaries" (1).

In his analysis, Mbembe also emphasizes the underlying connection between a wanderer and the space he/ she occupies. In his study, he further argues that "every subject is a wandering subject . . . What is important is where one ends up" (144). Thus, we see that the pertinence of the concept lies in the space or spatial groups associated with a specific geography. The path and the space that the wanderers occupy play a key role in the formation of their identity and resilience. The experiences of a wanderer in a particular space affect his ability to confront and endure uncertainties and other challenges. Thus, the idea of the relation between the resilience of wandering subjects and their space deserves to have attention in the studies of literary geographies. The Jewish community, mostly equated as the "quintessential diaspora" (Reis 41), aligns with the concept of a wanderer as they have seen a long history of exile, migration and cultural displacement. Arnold Ages, a Canadian Scholar, remarks in this regard that "the homelessness of Jews has been a leitmotiv in Jewish literature, art, culture, and of course, prayer" (Ages 10).

In contrast to numerous fictional works that often-delineated Jews as hapless victims, the novels from Kerala deviated from prevailing narratives, providing fresh perspectives on the Jewish experience at the hostland. In this article, I aim to examine the novel *The Saga of Muziris* (a Malayalam novel written by Sethu) to inspect the ways in which the space of Muziris provided a refugee-friendly environment for Jews and fostered their well-being during their residency. This space holds such significance that it is referred to as "the only safe haven in the history of the Jewish Diaspora" (Retrieved from Nandy 316). In this study, I attempt to read *The Saga of Muziris* as a text to elucidate how an environment of hospitality and sustained practices of cultural autonomy played a pivotal role in fostering their resilience and sense of belonging.

Resilience and Metropolitan Spaces of Refuge

Resilience is generally understood as a psychological attribute associated with the inner self (Grafton et al.). However, several critics argue that resilience is also a "social phenomenon" (Lenette et al. 2). The idea stems from the argument that a wanderer requires support from outside in the face of adversity, which contributes to resilience. As Ungar also argues, resilience is "the capacity of the individual's environment to provide access to health-enhancing resources in culturally relevant ways" (Ungar et al. 88). The social, economic and political circumstances subsequently affect the physical, emotional and intellectual well-being of a wanderer.

The idea of resilience reflects on varied prospects of thoughts in relation to refugees and their subsequent refuge. The studies on the idea of resilience, primarily associated with refugee communities (for instance, see Daud, af Klinteberg and Rydelieu; Van Acker et al.; Tippens) also provoke thoughts on the notion of the role of refuge as a space in the attainment of resilience. Further to this idea, in the study of exploration of the experiences of Afghan refugee children in Canada, Kanji and Cameron argue the role of "consistent support" in acquiring resilience (Kanji and Cameron 26). Thus, Internal resilience can be understood to be achieved through the right social support in terms of infrastructure, safety, and external assistance (Pulvirenti and Mason; Sukufe, Yurtbakan and Acarturk). These inferences reinforce the need to look into the spatial frameworks of refugees and the studies to understand how resilience is achieved through a positive environment.

However, the spatial engagements of refuge have profusely analyzed the setting of a metropolis into its framework. Most of the studies perceive the city as an "agent of refugee integration" (Doomernik and Ardon 91) and a hub of "cosmopolitan citizenship" (Oomen 121). The flux of numerous privileged and unprivileged sections to cities led to the cosmopolitan discussions of metropolitan cities (Warf). Cities with the advantage of sovereignty and autonomy over nation-states are a predominant metaphor for cosmopolitanism and hospitality.

Derrida, in his study on cosmopolitanism, introduces the idea of "cities of refuge" (4) as an embodiment of hospitality and of a "new cosmo*politics*" (Derrida 4). Derrida gives a central status to the cities as centres of "greater sovereignty" to provide an unbiased and "immediate response to crime, to violence and to persecution" (23). However, the refugee experiences in urban centres point towards discriminatory practices of spatial separation and exclusion.

For instance, Jews, the quintessential diaspora, have seen and suffered discrimination at many points of their refugee life. Hannah Arendt, in her essay "We Refugees", shares the refugee experiences of Jews in major metropolitan cities. She remarks, "In Paris we could not leave our homes after eight o' clock because we were Jews; but in Los Angeles we are restricted because we are enemy aliens" (270). In addition to this, the cities followed spatial separation as a method to keep the refugees separate from the resident communities. The concept of a ghetto came to be associated with a part of the city where Jews were forced to live (Wirth). The origin of the term is traced to Venice when the Jews were segregated and forced to reside in the street called the ghetto nuovo (Ravid; Davis), followed by other "measures including the compulsory wearing of yellow hats" (Coaffee, Murakami, and Rogers) during the beginning of the fifteenth century. The city of Frankfort also exhibited unjust treatment against the Jews, primarily during the fourteenth century. The medieval Jewish quarters in the European cities of Paris and Berlin were built "because Jews were not allowed, before emancipation, to live anywhere else in the European city" (Laguerre 5). The practices of ethnic disintegration continue to affect many immigrant groups across Western cities, even during the twentieth and twenty-first centuries (Xu, Cutler, Glaeser, and Vigdor).

The colonial Indian metropolises, despite being considered as the hub of cosmopolitan spirit and hospitality, have shown intolerance towards the immigrant communities from different parts of the world. Still, it is the metropolitan cities, predominantly Mumbai, that get the attention for representing the site of refuge and cosmopolitanism. Mumbai's recognition as a cosmopolitan city extends from anglophone fiction to their critical and scholarly renditions. In the postcolonial sensibility, Bombay continues to be hailed as the "maximum city" (Mehta) and the "sine qua non of the postcolonial city" (Ashcroft 497) over the other Indian cities. On the contrary, Bombay has also been the focal point of the discussions of the decline of cosmopolitanism as well. The studies on the rise of Hindu Cosmopolitanism (Waghmore), crime (McFarlane; Soni; Khanna) and intolerance throw light into the visible parochial mindset that the metropolitan spaces had positioned against. But even in the decline of cosmopolitan order as well, Mumbai continues to be a "metaphor for modern India" (Patel and Thorner). Other critics like Anjali Bharadwaj Datta also reflect on the community-based segregation of refugees in Delhi during 1947 (152). By looking at the cities of Kolkata and Istanbul, Basu and Asci argue on the necessity to rethink the twentieth century cities of refuge, considering the increasing poverty and violence.

There are many other non- metropolitan refugee spaces in India, which are seldom brought into the theoretical discussions. This study sustains this thought of the need to look at alternative or provincial sites of centres of refuge other than metropolises.

Provincializing Cities of Refuge

One method to incorporate other spaces into the fabric of cities of refuge is by provincializing the concept of cities of refuge. Provincializing, as Dipesh Chakrabarty argues, is a project to decentralize and renew European thought "from and for the margins" (16). Though it has been primarily studied for critiquing postcoloniality's universal engagements with history, it is a method to critique the majoritarian spatialities of postcolonial scholarship. To expand the frame of postcolonial spatialities, we need other frameworks of smaller cities, towns, villages and neighbourhoods. As Geeta Kapur writes, "It is better, perhaps, to 'provincialise' Europe - and not in vengeance or caprice, but by setting up alternative paradigms wherein our understand of cosmopolitanism, internationalism and globalisation is recurrently complicated" (34). Thus, we need further paradigms to add to the theorisations of spatiality on the grounds of refuge, cosmopolitanism and resilience.

Emily Johansen proposes the applicability of the idea of cities of refuge to wider frameworks of "the small city, the rural community and the neighborhood" (Johansen 13). Some studies already offer a glimpse into refugee life in small cities. Pablo S Bose, in his study of refugee settlements, attempts to look at the refugee population of small cities and suburban towns, including Burlington (83) and Winooski (121), to argue how they have contributed to the economic and social development of the space. Stacey Haugan focuses on the positive outcomes of Syrian Refugee integration in the rural communities of Canada, where they "benefit from the social capital, economic opportunities, and affordable housing options" (Haugen 61). In the Indian postcolonial sensibility, we need varied geographies of small cities and neighbourhoods to be added into this frame of thought. Since the precolonial times, India has witnessed an influx of refugees who arrived through the sea routes of the Indian Ocean. The Indian Ocean played a key role in linking different trade routes and promoting the mobility of people. It produced a modernity in cosmopolitan thought as it facilitated the interaction of different people of different communities. Hofmeyr refers to the Indian Ocean as a "site par excellence of alternative modernities; those formations of modernity that have taken shape in an archive of deep and layered existing social and intellectual traditions" (13).

Cochin, one of the two-tier cities of Kerala, traces the history of its many groups of inhabitants to the precolonial times when the Indian ocean opened paths for different communities to reach this port city. Cochin can be seen as an apt location to add to the spatial theorisation of refuge as it has seen the presence of wanderers from different communities since pre-colonial times. A European colony for 444 years, Cochin has been a hub of maritime trade since its birth. Despite having a rich cosmopolitan history, Kochi is rarely represented in the mainstream discussions of spatiality. Ashis Nandy, in his ethnographic study on Cochin, "reject[s] history as a guide to the 'living past' of Cochin" (298) and attempts to connect Cochin's present with its mythic past.

Salman Rushdie's *The Moor's Last Sigh* was one of the first novels to acquaint the literary geography of Cochin with the repertoire of Indian English fiction. After the publication of the novel, a lot of Malayalam novels attempted to represent Cochin's history and cosmopolitan legacy. *Lanthan Batheriyile*

Luthiniyakal by N S Madhavan is one of the finest examples of geographical narratives that map the cultural, political and subaltern history of Cochin. **Sethumadahavan's novel *Marupiravi*,** translated into English as *The Saga of Muziris*, is one of the first novels from Kerala to consciously chronicle the history of the arrival of Jews during the ancient times of Muziris. Muziris, an ancient harbour town located in the region of Kerala, India, served as a prominent hub of commercial activities and trade interactions during the ancient and medieval periods, facilitating the trade linkages between India, the Roman Empire, the Middle East, and East Asia. Flourishing in prosperity, this city got submerged beneath the ground as the result of a catastrophic flood during the fourteenth century. Muziris also assumes a crucial role as the precursor to the contemporary port of Cochin and as Ashis Nandy remarks, "In Cochini imagination, Cochin is the rebirth of that dead, ancient, cultural capital of Kerala" (304).

The Saga of Muziris, thus, is a glimpse of the events revolving around the arrivals and the sustenance of varied cultures through centuries of rebirths and revival of spaces. The choice of the original title in Malayalam, 'Marupiravi' (where '*maru*-' denotes 're-' and '*piravi*' denotes 'birth'), serves as an important allusion to the resurgence and rebirth of the once-lost space and the rich cultural history of the magnificent ancient harbour town, Muziris. Through a sustained and methodical narrative, the novel becomes an exemplary model of historical writing, striving to document the profound historical legacy of the region.

A Context of the Novel

The Saga of Muziris is a narrative that delves into the 2,000-year-old history of the port of Muziris, tracing its transformation over time. The story unfolds in the twenty-first century when residents of Pattanam, a village in the district of Ernakulam, discover foreign artefacts, sparking intrigue about Muziris' pertinence in Asia's maritime history. Aravindan, a former resident of Pattanam and the protagonist, decides to write about Muziris and its evolution from a thriving port to its decline and its metaphorical rebirth with the emergence of Cochin as an affluent port. Divided into four parts, the novel takes the readers through several historical periods, exploring the elements that contributed to Cochin's growth. The protagonist, through the method of novel within a novel, sets the narrative in the fourth century Muziris, where one witnesses the shift of an agrarian society to a bustling port city with the arrival of traders. The novel also focuses on the history of Jews in Kochi, acknowledging their contributions to the city and their role as early settlers. The novel concludes in the twenty-first century, where the progenies of the Muziris era sustain the commercial and cosmopolitan legacy. Aravindan metaphorically links the Vallarpadam Container

Transhipment Terminal to Muziris, visualizing a rebirth of the ancient city in modern-day Kochi. Throughout the narrative, Aravindan interweaves multiple time periods to showcase the diverse and vibrant history of Kochi and its connection to its ancient past. The ensuing sections of the article explore how the narrative illustrates Cochin as a 'city of refuge', emphasizing its enduring hospitality and tolerance towards the Jewish community and the deep connection the Jewish community develops with the land, linking it to their ancestral homeland.

Cochin: The Land of Others

Sethu's novel is a reminder of what Cochin is. As TV Sajeev opines, it "is not where one belongs, but where the other belongs"(100), highlighting its rich cultural tapestry. The rise of Cochin as a major port is marked by the migration and settlement of multiple communities, including the Jewish traders, who were embraced by the "hospitality of the benevolent kings and the amiable people" (Jacob 4). In his study of Cochin, E P Unny observes that "The Jews who successively fled serial repression all the way from Europe and the Middle East were already among the prominent subjects of the Kochi King" (98). Ashis Nandy, in his study, delves into another distinctive group of Jews in Cochin known as the "Meshuhrarim", meaning "freed slaves" (313), who were also integral members of the community. Edna Fernandes, in her research on the Jews in Kerala, states how the Jewish diaspora "never knew persecution in their adopted land. Instead, they were feted by Kerala's rajas as foreign kings, lavished with land, privilege, and autonomy" (14). Moreover, J.B. Segal, in his historical work, mentions that "There were many Jews in the army of the Rajah of Cochin, and it is likely that they were members of the Black section of the community" (134).

This inclusive narrative of hospitality finds expression in Sethu's novel, *The Saga of Muziris*. The novel offers valuable insights into Cochin's multifaceted and historically rooted tradition of fostering a welcoming environment for diverse communities. In the novel, the narrator remembers this benevolence of the Kochi kings after the submergence of Muziris port and remarks that "the king of Kochi not only welcomed the Jewish merchants who approached him, he allotted land right next to the palace for a market, which soon became a busy place. Since the market place was smaller than the one at Kodungallur, it became Kochangadi or the small market. A synagogue was raised without much delay" (290). When the legacy of trade history of the port of Muziris attracted different communities to the land in the beginning, Cochin became a place where they took refuge at times of social, economic, political and natural crises. The cosmopolitan space of Cochin led to stretching the duration of their habitation through centuries of political changes.

The novel also remembers Joseph Rabban, a Jewish merchant from Syria, who was made the regional chieftain in return for the loyalty that Rabban had shown at the time of longstanding conflict between the kingdoms of the Cheras and Cholas, characterized by recurrent warfare. Following the Chera king's defeat at Vizhinjam (a harbour town in present-day Thiruvananthapuram), the Cheras were forced to retreat. Concurrently, during a strategic meeting of chieftains organized by the Cholas, Joseph Rabban offered initial assistance to the Chera king. Rabban pledged his armed and financial resources to help the Cheras. In appreciation of this admirable display of loyalty, the Chera king granted Rabban the status of an autonomous principality, bestowing him rulership over the territory of Anchuvannam. Foreign visitors to the land at the time referred to Joseph Rabban as "the King of Shingli" (289). This title held significant esteem for the Jewish community, who had encountered dispersion and the loss of their ancestral lands. Joseph Rabban, alternatively known as Chiryanandan, denoting "the Pride of Syria" (289), indicated ancestral origins tracing back to the Syrian region. Rabban is believed to have given "a copper plate that included seventy-two rights" (288) in ruling the region allotted to him.

This tradition of Kingdoms' expression of loyalty and faithfulness towards the Jews is visible throughout the novel. Cochin is painted as a setting where those who arrived as refugees stayed on through generations, retaining their individuality while joining the mainstream life of the land. This unique blend of diversity and integration fostered an environment of hospitality and tolerance. Sethu depicts the communal coexistence and cosmopolitanism that existed in Cochin, where the government and the people did not perceive the Jews as outsiders. Aravindan reflects, "Incidentally, our village was one of the earliest settlements of Jews on our western coast, and we had many Jewish friends in our class" (53). Bezalel, a migrant from Cochin, also reminisces about their peaceful existence, stating, "Actually, we had no problems here, ever. Neither the government nor the people saw us as outsiders" (295). Moreover, government policies and institutions in Cochin demonstrated remarkable inclusivity and secularism. The author writes, "The rulers of Kochi had reserved seats for Jewish representatives in their legislative assembly. Two seats each were reserved in the college and civil service also" (295). The novel praises Kochi Kings and the government for being supportive of the traders and migrants from different parts of the world. Aravindan, the protagonist, remembers his childhood when Jewish students had a separate Hebrew teacher and special holidays on Saturdays to attend the Sabbath.

Sethu brings the spatial metaphor of the Kottayil Kovilakam as an illustrious example of religious harmony among diverse communities. It is an area in Cochin where there is a church, mosque, temple and synagogue within a short radius. Aravindan, as an old resident of the village, recalls the enchanting symphony of the temple's conch, the mosque's muezzin, and the church bells. He opines that the village's peaceful coexistence amidst the tumultuous religious conflicts was truly remarkable during the time. He continues to parallel Cochin's cosmopolitanism against the communal riots that occurred in the northern states. The narrator remarks,

> During his Bombay days, when he heard the stories of his friends from the northern states, he realised that this was nothing—whole villages had been burned in the name of caste; wells, water sources, schools and even hospitals were known by their castes; there were panchayats, the village councils, that ordered young people who married outside the caste to be killed, inhuman tribal elders who prided themselves on their castes—the world had changed so much, and yet these places still lived in some dark ages. But Kochi had not been like that. The churches, synagogues and mosques inside the area of the Kottayil Kovilakam said a different story, a story of unity, of tolerance, of goodness (89).

When the critics discuss the death of cosmopolitanism in Bombay (Godrej), Cochin is still hailed as a space "where the precolonial traditions of cultural pluralism refuse to die" (Nandy 295). In Nandy's study, Elias, a Jew member in Cochin, comments to Nandy on his decision to stay in Cochin as he finds it to be "a city of immigrants" (321). Nandy further expands this argument and states that "Cochin belongs to the Jews as much as it belongs to the others" (321).

Cochin: The Interim Homeland and Beyond

The notion of home has been a fascinating area of discussion which has invited multiple perceptions. Home is understood to be "an impossible place, an utopia" (Bronfen) and a "mythic place of desire in the diasporic imagination" (Brah 188). On the contrary, home is also perceived as the "lived experience of a locality" (Brah 188-189). The life of Jews, with whom the quintessential notion of diaspora is associated, has been one of recurrent migrations and rootlessness. Robert Cohen argues that "diaspora signified a collective trauma, a banishment, where one dreamed of home but lived in exile" (ix). Edna Fernandes argues that "For the Jews, Kerala was always meant to be no more than an interim homeland, a sanctuary until they could return to the land of their forefathers, ending their spiritual dislocation" (Fernandes, 48). *The Saga of Muziris* offers a perspective that Cochin stood as an in-between possibility of a homeland and a hostland for the Jewish immigrants. The Jewish community, despite being offered a comfortable life in Cochin, chose to leave and work hard in a new place due to their sense of nationality arising from religion. Aravindan reflects, "That is where the Jews from Cochin (Kochi) are different. They had grown up without undergoing any travails of persecution. They gave up a comfortable life here to go to a new place and work hard at things they did not know, only because of a sense of nationality arising from religion" (150).

Aravindan attempts to opine that the migration of the Jews from Cochin to Israel, following the incident of the independence of Israel in 1948, was not a decision taken lightly, as it entailed confirming their religious obligation while abandoning their cherished homeland. Moreover, there was fear of going to an unknown and alien land. Aravindan recalls his friend from the Jew community who shared, "For the Jews who lived here in comfort, the transplanting was likely to be more difficult. They did not know what awaited them in the new land. Lots of people had doubts in their minds. The fear of being isolated was stronger than the call of the Holy Land" (286). Beyond religious, familial and social ties, a unique bond united the Jews to the land. Acknowledging the immense security provided by this close-knit circle, transcending boundaries and expressing their sentiments, one of them laments, "Now that it's time to go, I wish we didn't have to go" (286). Aravindan recalls that the collective departure of Jews weighed heavily on them, as they acknowledged the goodwill of the people and the sense of community they felt in Cochin, never feeling like outsiders. Amidst the emotional struggle, many Jews consoled themselves, affirming, "We are not going forever. We are only going away to come back again" (287). They acknowledge that their roots in the soil could never be severed, and the call of their ancestral land would persistently beckon them. The novel portrays the departure of the Jews as a very sad incident as they express gratitude, recognizing that their connection to the land was enduring and that they would someday return, even as visitors and spectators. Seemon, one of Aravindan's friends, shares the deep reverence he has for the soil that once provided sanctuary to their ancestors resonated within their hearts. The novel expresses that Cochin stood as an interim homeland for the Jewish refugees, offering them a sense of security and deep-rooted attachment to the land. Despite their eventual relocation to Israel, the Jews of Cochin acknowledged the enduring impact of their time in the city and expressed their desire to return one day, appreciating Cochin's significant place in their collective memory and history.

Conclusion

The cities of refuge have been a very prominent idea in the fictional and theoretical engagement of cosmopolitanism. However, many regional spaces with incredible histories of hospitality are mostly ignored in the scholarship of refugee spaces. The spaces where the refugees inhabit contribute to their resilience and identity formation. Thus, it is significant to provincialize the concept of the cities of refuge and look at the different possible spaces other than metropolises. We need other local and provincial spaces in the frame of refugee spaces which acknowledge their presence and contributions through different practices. This article is thus an attempt to provincialize the concept of cities of refuge and look at other spaces like Cochin to prove how its history and geography are unique and deserve more attention than the cliched theorisations of metropolitan spatiality. Sethu's novel, *The Saga of Muziris*, is a perfect entry point towards the project of provincializing the theorizations of the literary geographies of cities of refuge. The novel broadens the scope of perspectives on the generalized notions of hostland and exile and offers alternative histories and geographies for a 'homable' hostland.

Works Cited

Ages, Arnold. *The Diaspora Dimension.* The Hague, 1973.

Arendt, Hannah. "We Refugees." *The Jewish Writings*, edited by Jerome Kohn and Ron H Feldman, Shocken Books, 2007, pp. 264–274.

Bose, Pablo S. *Refugees in New Destinations and Small Cities.* Springer Nature, 2020.

Brah, Avtar. *Cartographies of Diaspora.* Routledge, 1996.

Bronfen, Elisabeth. *Home in Hollywood: The Imaginary Geography of Cinema.* Columbia University Press, 2004.

Bulchandani, Saanthia. 2021. *Complex Cosmopolitanism?: The Transformation of Public Space in Colonial and Postcolonial Bombay.* Penguin, 2021.

Chakrabarty, Dipesh. *Provincializing Europe.* New Jersey: Princeton University Press, 2000.

Coaffee, Jon, et al. *The Everyday Resilience of the City: How Cities Respond to Terrorism and Disaster.* Palgrave Macmillian, 2009.

Cohen, Robert. *Global Diasporas: An Introduction,* Routledge, 1997.

Cutler, David M., Edward L. Glaeser and Jacob L. Vigdor. "Is the Melting Pot Still Hot? Explaining the Resurgence of Immigrant Segregation." *Review of Economics and Statistics*, vol. 90, no. 3, 2008, pp. 478–497, https://doi.org/10.1162/rest.90.3.478

Datta, Anjali Bhardwaj. "Genealogy of a Partition City: War, Migration and Urban Space in Delhi." *South Asia: Journal of South Asian Studies*, vol. 42, no. 1, 2 Jan. 2019, pp. 152–169, https://doi.org/10.1080/00856401.2019.1557028.

Daud, Atia, Britt af Klinteberg, and Per-Anders Rydelius. "Resilience and Vulnerability among Refugee Children of Traumatized and Non-Traumatized Parents." *Child and Adolescent Psychiatry and Mental Health*, vol. 2, no. 1, 2008, https://doi.org/10.1186/1753-2000-2-7.

Davis, Robert C., and Benjamin Ravid, editors. *The Jews of early modern Venice.* JHU Press, 2001.

Derrida, Jacques. *On Cosmopolitanism and Forgiveness.* Translated by Mark Dooley and Michael Hughes, Routledge, 1997.

Doomernik, Jeroen, and Djoeke Ardon. "The City as an Agent of Refugee Integration." *Urban Planning*, vol. 3, no. 4, 20 Dec. 2018, pp. 91–100, https://doi.org/10.17645/up.v3i4.1646

Fernandes, Edna. 2008. *The Last Jews of Kerala: The Two Thousand Year History of India's Forgotten Jewish Community.* Skyhorse Publishing Inc., 2008.

Godrej, Farah. "The tales we tell: Bombay, Mumbai and I." *Critical Review of International Social and Political Philosophy,* vol. 25, no. 5, 2022, pp. 703–722. https://doi.org/10.1080/13698230.2021.1881740.

Grafton, Eileen, et al. "Resilience: The Power Within." *Oncology Nursing Forum,* vol. 37, no. 6, 1 Nov. 2010, pp. 698–705, https://doi.org/10.1188/10.onf.698-705.

Haugen, Stacey. 2019. ""We Feel Like We're Home": The Resettlement and Integration of Syrian Refugees in Smaller and Rural Canadian Communities." *Refuge: Canada's Journal on Refugees,* vol. 35, no. 2, 2019, pp. 53–63, https://doi.org/10.7202/1064819ar.

Hofmeyr, Isabel. "The Black Atlantic Meets the Indian Ocean: Forging New Paradigms of Transnationalism for the Global South–Literary and Cultural Perspectives." *Social dynamics,* vol. 33, no. 2, 2007, pp. 3–32.

Jacob, Asha Susan. "Aliyah: The Last Jew in the Village—A Poetics of the History of Jews in Kerala." *South Asian Review,* vol. 42, no. 3, 2021, pp. 218–233.

Johansen, Emily. *Cosmopolitanism and Place: Spatial Forms in Contemporary Anglophone Literature,* Palgrave Macmillan, 2014.

Kanji, Zeenatkhanu, and Brenda L. Cameron. "Exploring the Experiences of Resilience in Muslim Afghan Refugee Children." *Journal of Muslim Mental Health,* vol. 5, no. 1, 31 Mar. 2010, pp. 22–40, https://doi.org/10.1080/15564901003620973

Kapur, Geeta. "Kochi- Muziris Biennale: Site Imaginaries." *Kochi- Muziris Biennale (2012- Catalogue Book),* D C Books, 2012.

Khanna, Stuti. "Crime, Media, and the People: "Murder Most Foul" and City Mythologies." *South Asian Review,* vol. 36, no. 2, 2015, pp. 131–146, https://doi.org/10.1080/02759527.2015.11933022

Laguerre, Michel S. *Global Neighborhoods: Jewish Quarters in Paris, London, and Berlin.* SUNY Press, 2008.

Lenette, Caroline, et al. "Everyday Resilience: Narratives of Single Refugee Women with Children." *Qualitative Social Work: Research and Practice,* vol. 12, no. 5, 11 June 2012, pp. 637–653, https://doi.org/10.1177/1473325012449684.

Madhavan, N.S. *Lanthan Batheriyile Luthiniyakal.* D C Books, 2010.

Mbembe, Achille. *Critique of Black Reason.* Duke University Press, 2017.

Mbembe, Achille., & Mitsch, R. H. "Life, Sovereignty, and Terror in the fiction of Amos Tutuola." *Research in African Literatures,* vol. 34, no. 4, 2003, pp. 1–26. https://www.jstor.org/stable/4618325.

Mehta, Suketu. *Maximum City: Bombay Lost and Found.* Penguin Random House, 2004.

McFarlane, Colin. "Postcolonial Bombay: Decline of a Cosmopolitanism City?" *Environment and Planning D: Society and Space,* vol. 26, no. 3, 2008, pp. 480–499. https://doi.org/10.1068/dcos6

Nandy, Ashis. *An Ambiguous Journey to the City: The Village and Other Odd Ruins of the Self in the Indian Imagination.* Oxford University Press, 2001.

Nandy, Ashis. "Time Travel to a Possible Self: Searching for the Alternative Cosmopolitanism of Cochin." *Japanese Journal of Political Science*, vol. 1, no. 2, 2000, pp. 295–327. https://doi.org/10.1017/S1468109900002061

Oomen, Barbara. "Cities of Refuge Rights, Culture and the Creation of Cosmopolitan Citizenship." *Cultures, Citizenship and Human Rights*, edited by Rosemarie Buikema et al., Routledge, 2019, pp. 121–136.

Patel, Sujata and Alice Thorner, editors. *Bombay: Metaphor for Modern India*, Oxford University Press, 1996.

Pulvirenti, Mariastella; Mason, Gail. "Resilience and Survival: Refugee Women and Violence." *Current Issues in Criminal Justice*, vol. 23, no. 1, 2011, pp. 37–52. doi:10.1080/10345329.2011.12035908.

Ravid, Benjamin CI. "The First Charter of the Jewish Merchants of Venice, 1589." *AJS review*, vol. 1, 1976, pp. 187–222. https://www.jstor.org/stable/1486343.

Reis, Michele. "Theorizing Diaspora: Perspectives on "Classical" and "Contemporary" Diaspora." *International Migration*, vol. 42 no. 2, 2004, pp. 41–60.

Sajeev, T.V. "Kochi, the Other City." *Cities in Kerala, Actually Small Towns*, edited by B Natarajan, Marg Publications, 2008, pp. 88–103.

Segal, Judah Benzion. *A History of the Jews of Cochin*, Vallentine Mitchell, 1993.

Simmel, Georg. "The Stranger." *Georg Simmel on Individuality and Social Forms*, edited by Donald N Levine, University of Chicago Press, 2011, pp. 143–149.

Soni, Tripti. "Spatialization, Crime and Making of Bombay, India: A Geocritical Study of Narcopolis, Maximum City and Shantaram." *GeoJournal*, vol. 87, 2021, pp. 2239–2253.

Tippens, Julie A. "Urban Congolese Refugees' Social Capital and Community Resilience During a Period of Political Violence in Kenya: A Qualitative Study." *Journal of Immigrant & Refugee Studies*, vol. 18, no. 1, 2020, pp. 42–59.

Ungar Michael, et al. "Unique Pathways to Resilience Across Cultures." *Adolescence*, vol. 42, No. 166, 2007, pp. 287–310. PMID: 17849937.

Van Acker, K., Groeninck, M., Geldof, D., Meurs, P., & Wiewauters, C. "Holding Hope and Mastering the Possible: Mapping Resilient Moves of Asylum-Seeking and Refugee Families Post Arrival." *European Journal of Social Work*, vol. 26, no. 3, 2022, pp. 1–14.

Waghmore, Suryakant. "Community, Not Humanity: Caste Associations and Hindu Cosmopolitanism in Contemporary Mumbai." *South Asia: Journal of South Asian Studies*, vol. 42, no. 2, 2019, pp.375–393.

Warf, Barney. "Global Cities, Cosmopolitanism, and Geographies of Tolerance." *Urban Geography*, vol. 36, no. 6, 2015, pp. 927–946.

Wirth, Louis, editor. *The Ghetto*. Transaction Publishers, 1956.

Xu, Dafeng. "Surname-Based Ethnicity and Ethnic Segregation in the Early Twentieth Century US." *Regional Science and Urban Economics*, vol. 77, 2019, pp. 1–19.

Chapter 3

In Search of a Home:
A Queer Hero's Quest to Belong

Aleena Achamma Paul

IIT Ropar, India

Abstract

This paper examines the confluence of trauma and heroism in Ursula K. Le Guin's novel, *The Telling* (2000), and further expands on the role of travel as a coping mechanism for individuals experiencing trauma, emphasising its potential for healing and self-discovery. The novel follows the protagonist, Sutty, a gay anthropologist who is sent on a mission as an observer to the fictional planet called Aka. The story delves into the intersections of trauma, travel, and heroism as Sutty navigates a totalitarian regime that suppresses traditional customs, drawing parallels with historical events such as the *Great Leap Forward* and the *Cultural Revolution* in Maoist China. Sutty's character is analysed as a wandering hero, drawing parallels with archetypal figures like Odysseus and Don Quixote. The chapter reads her journey as a quest for knowledge, understanding, and self-discovery as she confronts new cultures and challenges her assumptions. The paper also delves into the changing perceptions of 'home' for Sutty, exploring how trauma reshapes her connection to her childhood home and her subsequent quest for a new sense of belonging to Aka.

Keywords: Healing, Heroism, Home, Self-Discovery, Trauma

***

Introduction

The American sci-fi writer Ursula K. Le Guin has produced an extensive body of work that explores themes of gender, race, politics, and the human condition. She has consciously and consistently subverted and re-imagined dominant social, cultural and political structures through her writings to offer powerful commentaries on contemporary society. As the daughter of an anthropologist and a writer, Le Guin was introduced to a multitude of cultures, languages and myths (prominently Norse and Greek) from a very young age, and this influence is quite evident in her writings. Several of her works also reflect the influence of Taoist principles of duality and Jungian concepts of dream and shadow, which were a formative part of her life (Spivack 6). Additionally, her writing was characterised by its exploration of themes of power, identity, travel and social justice, as can be witnessed in her novel *The Telling* (2000).

The Telling is one of the many novels making up the *Hainish Cycle*, one of Le Guin's best-known science-fiction series. The novel follows the protagonist, Sutty, who is a gay Ekumen observer sent from Earth to the fictional planet of Aka to experience and document the rustic way of life on the planet. Ekumen is a galactic federation of human-inhabited worlds that engages in trade and exchange of ideas/technologies. Sutty, as a researcher had learnt of the way of living or religion in Aka called the "Telling." However, as Sutty reaches the planet, it is nothing like the one her studies had taught her to expect. A totalitarian, secularist government—different from the one she knew on Earth yet familiar in its attitudes— had taken over and imposed a language to be spoken by all, and any instances of the religious and cultural symbols of the old way were banned. How Sutty navigates her way through this challenging situation and attempts to preserve the ancient indigenous culture forms the crux of the novel.

The story rests on references to historical events; more specifically, the novel draws on the devastating consequences of the Great Leap Forward[1] (1958-60) and the Cultural Revolution[2] (1966-76) under the leadership of Chairman Mao Zedong (Smil 1619). Social, economic and cultural regulations imposed by the People's Republic of China, which were meant to reconstruct the country from an agrarian economy into a communist society, instead of stimulating the economy, caused mass starvation and famine (Li and Yang, 2005, 841). In the

---

[1] According to Wei Li and Dennis Tao Yang (2005), The Great Leap Forward was an economic and social movement launched by the Communist Party of China in 1958 which was meant to reinvent the country as an industrial economy rather than an agrarian economy. However, this movement failed and resulted in the largest famine in human history (841). While officially, the cause for the failure of the movement was attributed to bad weather, Li and Yang identified numerous policies such as reduced work incentives and curbing of labour rights among others as reasons for this tragedy (842).

[2] The Cultural Revolution, also known as the Great Proletarian Cultural Revolution (1966-1976) was launched by Mao Zedong to preserve and realise his version of communism after the failure of the Great Leap Forward (Lieberthal, 2023). Mass, youth-led paramilitary groups called Red Guards were formed who attacked "all traditional values and 'bourgeois' things" (Lieberthal) and this period has since been dubbed as the "ten-year turmoil" by historians (Ning, 2015).

novel, Le Guin draws parallels between Maoist China and the totalitarian government of Aka, as both insisted on the despotic suppression of traditional customs in the name of "Maoist-Marxist orthodoxy" (Thrall 199) and modernity, respectively. While social justice and preservation of tradition and culture are obvious concerns in *The Telling*, another focus of the novel is on trauma, especially Sutty's losses. Sutty decides to undertake the mission to Aka after the death of her partner in a terrorist bombing by an anti-gay religious extremist outfit. Sutty is well aware that since her mission involves space travel, she will not see her family again as travelling lightyears would take decades. She leaves behind her familiar and painful present to get away from her trauma. The chapter will focus on this aspect of the novel and study the correlation between trauma, travelling and heroism.

Trauma, Travel and Heroism

In the novel, the reasons for Sutty to leave behind Earth are multi-faceted. First and foremost, Sutty is running away from her trauma of losing her partner. Science fiction has provided a unique platform for exploring the impact of traumatic experiences on individuals and communities and how heroism can emerge in response to these challenges. Science fiction has also allowed authors to examine the impact of trauma on a large scale, often depicting entire worlds or civilisations that have been traumatised by war, environmental disasters, or other catastrophic events. Citing several science fiction movies as examples, Cyndy Hendershot notes in "Trauma to Paranoia: Nuclear Weapons, Science Fiction, and History" (1999) that "a paranoiac response to the cultural trauma caused by the reality and threat of nuclear destruction, and the way that such paranoia is reflected in *both fictional and non-fictional* works" (74, Italics in original). One of the most influential examples of trauma and heroism in American science fiction literature is Octavia Butler's *Parable of the Sower* (1993). The novel is set in a dystopian future where society has collapsed due to environmental degradation and social unrest. The protagonist, Lauren, is a young woman with hyper-empathy syndrome, which causes her to feel the physical pain and emotions of others. Despite the trauma she experiences, Lauren becomes a leader and a symbol of hope for her community, creating a new religion and guiding her followers to safety.

Another example of the intersection of trauma and heroism in American science fiction literature can be found in the works of Ursula K. Le Guin. In her novel *The Left Hand of Darkness* (1969), the protagonist, Genly Ai, is a human envoy sent to a planet inhabited by an androgynous species. Genly faces many challenges, including the trauma of being an outsider in a foreign world and the struggle to gain the trust of the planet's inhabitants. Despite these challenges, Genly ultimately demonstrates heroism through his willingness to learn from the planet's inhabitants and to work towards understanding and acceptance. Science fiction literature has also explored the impact of trauma on humankind as a whole as can be evidenced in Orson Scott Card's *Ender's Game* (1985). In this novel, humanity is at war with an alien species known as the Formics. The protagonist, Ender Wiggin, is a young genius who is recruited to join a training program for future military leaders. Ender faces many challenges, including the trauma of being forced to fight in a war at such a young age. Despite these challenges, Ender ultimately becomes a hero by leading humanity to victory in the war. Writers have used science fiction to explore the impact of traumatic experiences on individuals and communities and to examine how heroism can emerge in response to these challenges. Science fiction has allowed authors to depict large-scale trauma, providing a unique perspective on how societies can be impacted by war, environmental degradation, and other catastrophic events. Through their characters, authors have demonstrated the resilience and strength of individuals and communities in the face of trauma, highlighting the potential for heroism in the most challenging of circumstances.

This is also where the confluence of trauma and heroism happens with travelling. Trauma can occur as a result of a range of experiences, from natural disasters to physical and emotional abuse. Travelling, on the other hand, is often associated with adventure, relaxation, and exploration. However, for those who have experienced trauma, travelling can be a way to cope with the aftermath and move towards healing. Philip Kotler and G.M. Armstrong argue in *Principles of Marketing* (1982) that a person might have internal or external motivations for deciding to travel. They argue that internal stimuli arise from personal needs that can be physiological, social, egocentric, safety and self-actualisation. Whereas, external stimuli result from publicity and promotion (131). Similarly, Graham Dann points out in the article "Anomie, ego-enhancement and Tourism" (1977) that people travel to escape from daily routines and solitude (185). Furthermore, Seppo E. Iso- Ahola argues in "Towards a social psychology of recreational travel" (2006) that,

> It is shown that like leisure behaviour in general, recreational travel is a dialectical optimizing process, in which two forces simultaneously influence a person: the desire to leave the personal and/or interpersonal environment behind oneself *and* the desire to pursue or gain certain personal and/or interpersonal rewards. This process is dialectical in the sense that the person has to solve the contradiction between the need for novelty and familiarity to achieve optimally arousing experiences. It is also optimizing in the sense that the individual aims at an optimal amount and quality of contact with others, to shut oneself off from

others at one time and to open oneself up to interpersonal contacts at another time (45, Italics in original).

Interestingly, Wee and Mokhtarian correlate the connection between travel and escapism in "Escape Theory: Explaining a Negative Motivation to Travel" (2023) and note that "…people sometimes travel at least partly because they want to be away *from* a given place, and people might prefer *not* to quickly travel to destination…. nor to be easily accessible by others" (2, Italics in original). This observation can be extended to this paper to view travel as a powerful tool for individuals who have experienced trauma, as it provides an opportunity to escape the familiar and immerse oneself in new experiences. Travelling can help individuals break free from the triggers and reminders of their traumatic experiences and gain perspective on their situation. Being in a new environment can help individuals feel a sense of freedom and control over their lives, which can be especially valuable for those who have experienced trauma. Furthermore, travelling can be an opportunity for individuals to engage in self-care and promote healing. Taking a break from daily stressors and responsibilities can be a much-needed break for those who are recovering from trauma. Travelling can offer individuals the chance to engage in activities that promote relaxation and well-being, such as meditation or spending time in nature.

Adding to the previous argument, in *The Heroine's Journey* (2013), Jungian psychotherapist Maureen Murdock, while discussing the female hero's journey, remarks that the female hero rejects her own body and tries to identify with the masculine and constantly tries to measure up to the male-defined standards of success, thus resulting in a "mother/daughter split" or the "deep feminine wound" (17). What Sutty experiences is similar to this wound, except it is not her femininity that she is rejecting but her queerness. The trauma from the loss of her partner, the festering wound of queerness, and the loss of purpose leads Sutty to feel lost. She is, in a sense, homeless as she is devoid of the comforts she once had, including that of self-expression. As she is always monitored, she is advised to hide her sexual identity by her colleagues. She thinks to herself if her fear stems from "fear of being evil, or fear of being different" (*The Telling* 631). We can then surmise that, in the novel, Sutty uses travel as a means of escape from her traumas.

Sutty as a Wandering Hero

In literature, mythology, and folklore, typically, a wandering hero travels from place to place, usually with a specific quest or goal in mind. These heroes are often characterised by their lack of a fixed abode, their itinerant lifestyle, and their willingness to venture into unknown and dangerous territories. Wandering heroes appear in many different cultures and literary traditions. In Greek mythology, the hero Odysseus is a classic example of a wandering hero. After the Trojan War, Odysseus embarks on a ten-year journey home, encountering a series of obstacles and adventures along the way. In medieval literature, knights-errant were often portrayed as wandering heroes. These knights would travel across the countryside, seeking adventure and chivalrous deeds. The most famous example of a knight-errant is Don Quixote, the protagonist of Miguel de Cervantes' novel of the same name, published in 1605. In modern literature, the wandering hero archetype is still prevalent. For example, in J.R.R. Tolkien's *The Lord of the Rings* (1954), Frodo Baggins is a wandering hero who travels across Middle Earth to destroy the One Ring. Similarly, in Cormac McCarthy's novel *Blood Meridian* (1985), the character known as "the Kid" is a wandering hero who roams the American Southwest in search of fortune and adventure. Overall, the wandering hero is a timeless archetype that continues to fascinate and inspire readers and writers across cultures and literary traditions.

Coming back to the novel, while well aware that undertaking space travel would mean that she would be leaving behind everyone and everything familiar to her, Sutty decides to undertake the journey as she is in a metaphorical quest to find a safe space or a "home" that would allow her to reconnect with her "wounded queer" self, thus embodying the archetype of the wandering hero. Home has been and continues to be the locus for human development and identity. And therefore, there have been numerous attempts to define it. In "The House as Symbol of the Self" (2014), Clare Cooper thinks of home as a "symbol of self" (169) and that the interior of a home "symbolises the inhabitant's feelings about self" (170). Simply put, one considers home to be an extension of their self-, complete with memories and feelings attached to it. So, although the notion of domesticity has changed to a considerable degree over the years, both socially and structurally via egalitarian perceptions of social spheres, including tearing down the binaries of gender roles within the household, what has not essentially changed is that home remains to be described as a dwelling intricately tied to one's sense of self. It is often associated with safety, familiarity, memories and comfort. Home should ideally be a space where one can be their genuine self without fear of judgement.

Sutty talks about her earliest memories of her home called Pale in Vancouver. She finds the cold of the winter comforting. She says, "It went through her flimsy coat… it made you feel safe, the awful cold. She liked the North, the cold, the rain, the beautiful, dismal city" (*The Telling* 591). She describes the city as cold, wet and gloomy, and this is not a description one may normally use to describe something you like. But the safety and the warmth she felt during her childhood, in the presence of her family, make even the dismal city seem beautiful to her. On the other hand, Sutty's Aunt who has come to live with them from India, hates the city. She misses her husband and the life she had in India. She is described as sitting by the heater, "going away. Farther away all the time, but not by walking" (592). The aunt here tries to be home when away from home by keeping the memories of her husband and her life in the village alive through conversations.

Sociologist Craig Gurney expands on the conventional meanings associated with the concept of home in Meanings of Home and Home Ownership (1995) and points out that those attributes of a home that one would consider positive, say privacy, can also facilitate harmful, violent actions such as domestic violence, abuse or self-harm, and exacerbate loneliness and mental diseases (200). In the novel, as an adult, Sutty doesn't share the same feelings she had for her home as a child. After she loses her partner, Pao, to a university bombing, she suddenly feels lost and alone and loses the sense of hominess she had enjoyed earlier. Her home now becomes a familiar but painful reminder of her loss. When Sutty informs her mother of her plans to leave Earth, she responds, "This seems a rather good world to get off of, at present" (*The Telling* 594), recognising how it might be difficult for Sutty to continue in this socio-political climate and that too after the loss of her partner. Therefore, Sutty's motivation to travel is to distance herself as much as she can from this home she had created with Pao. As a student, Sutty had learnt that the Akan society was not hierarchically gendered and heterosexuality was not privileged. Given her current circumstances, she thought that Aka could serve as a haven for her. I quote, "It was her job. To live life after joy. Leave love and death behind her. Go on. Go alone and work" (609). However, upon arrival, another disappointment awaits her at Aka as the culture she was there to experience and document had been banned by its government, meaning she has now lost the haven she hoped for. Like on Earth, she will have to exercise caution and self-suppression to avoid being identified as queer.

Her journey takes her through unfamiliar terrain and introduces her to a society undergoing rapid change, forcing her to confront new ideas and challenge her assumptions. One of the key characteristics of the wandering hero is their lack of a fixed abode, and Sutty embodies this trait throughout the novel. She is constantly on the move, travelling from city to city and encountering new people and ideas along the way. Her journey takes her through diverse landscapes, from the lush forests of the countryside to freezing mountain ranges. Like many wandering heroes, Sutty is also on a quest for knowledge and understanding. She seeks to learn about Aka's culture and history, particularly the lost art of "Telling", a form of oral storytelling that has been suppressed by the planet's authoritarian government. Sutty's quest is not just a personal one, however. As a representative of the Ekumen, she is also tasked with bridging the cultural divide between her society and the people of Aka. As Sutty travels through Aka, she encounters a range of challenges and obstacles, both physical and intellectual. She is forced to confront her assumptions and biases about the planet's culture, and she struggles to navigate the complex political landscape of the society she encounters. Despite these challenges, Sutty remains committed to her quest, and her determination and perseverance are key to her success.

Ultimately, Sutty's journey is a journey of self-discovery. Through her encounters with the people of Aka, she comes to a deeper understanding of herself and her own society. She also gains a new appreciation for the power of storytelling and the importance of preserving cultural traditions and histories. By the end of the novel, Sutty has grown as a character, and her experiences have left a lasting impact on her worldview. As a traveller on a quest for knowledge and understanding, she navigates unfamiliar terrain, confronts new ideas, and challenges her assumptions. Through her perseverance and determination, she overcomes the obstacles in her path and emerges a stronger, more self-aware individual. *The Telling* is a testament to the power of the wandering hero archetype and the enduring appeal of stories about quests for knowledge and self-discovery[3]. After almost a year's wait, she is allowed to wander a village on her own and she discovers that there remain some pockets of cultural fossilisation deep within the mountains. In the village, she is welcomed by the natives to partake in their day-to-day lives. They share their stories and secrets with her. As she practices meditation and their way of life, she starts the process of healing from her traumas. The old ways, although practised secretly, created a space for Sutty to feel safe again. Her time in the village, its people and their culture reminds Sutty of her childhood, a time when she felt safe, carefree and happy. Le Guin writes, "Since she came to Okzat-Ozkat, she had slept well, without the long memory-excursions that had broken her nights... she woke up every night in the depths of the darkness and was back in the Pale" (639). She slowly starts shedding her fear and takes the bold decision to undertake a perilous journey to the mountains to retrieve the banned books. The journey is dangerous not only because it is physically challenging but also because, if discovered by the government, she would be executed. Nonetheless, she decides to do it because she and the rebels share similar experiences of exile and forced migration outside of an original home. The search for a 'home' that signifies a space for self-fulfilment and realisation of her queer identity is possible only through this difficult journey involving loss and gain.

---

[3] Quests for knowledge and thereby self-discovery is a common trope in heroic quests narratives from around the globe. For instance, pilgrim Dante's journey through Hell, Purgatory and Heaven in Dante Alighieri's *Divine Comedy* is a quest to uncover knowledge about the after-life and the nature of sin and redemption. In this novel, while uncovering and documenting the knowledge shared through *Telling*, Sutty realises the importance of her task as a researcher and accepts the challenge despite the dangers it presents. She discovers her integrity, dedication and strength during this quest.

As Mike Cadden notes in "Purposeful Movement Among People and Places: The Sense of Home in Ursula K. Le. Guin's Fiction for Children and Adults" (2000), "Movement is both health and home in Le Guin's fiction" (338). Cadden adds that Le Guin's characters attempt self-realisation through recognition of their role about the people and place they come across during their travel (338). It is through "dialogic and purposeful movement" of various characters that a sense of belonging is developed (338). Elizabeth Cummins remarks that in Le Guin's fiction, "journeying is an analogy for living; the process of going and returning, of fragmenting and unifying, is regenerating and unending" (154). The productive, never-ending journeys undertaken by Le Guin's characters show us that finding a home is never really a matter of fixing fragments or even of regenerating lapsed states; home is rather maintained through uninterrupted dialogue. Her characters find home when they resist silence and stasis as they move purposefully with the other characters across the spaces between sites. So, what it means to be home has been chaotically refashioned and continues to be reworked according to the needs of individuals who feel restricted by social constructions of homes or by traumatic events that deconstruct those concepts. (Garcia 11)

Conclusion

In *The Telling*, Sutty is a wandering hero whose journey to rediscover and preserve the ancient ways of storytelling and cultural heritage is an act of heroic resistance against oppressive forces. Additionally, the journey that she undertakes is an attempt on her part to escape from her trauma while simultaneously searching for a place of belonging or a home. She transforms from a librarian from Earth to a secret rebel upon discovering that the government of Aka has banned all books and stories that do not conform to their idea of progress and modernity; she sets out on a mission to find and record the lost stories of the Akans and to save them from being forgotten forever. Sutty's journey is a heroic one because she faces numerous challenges and obstacles in her quest to preserve the Akans' cultural heritage. She must navigate a society that is hostile to her and her ideas, where books and stories are considered dangerous and subversive. Sutty faces opposition from the government and the military, who see her as a threat to their power and authority. Despite these challenges, Sutty perseveres in her quest. She seeks out the few remaining storytellers and records their stories in secret. She also forms relationships with the Akans and learns about their culture and way of life. Sutty's journey is one of self-discovery as well, as she learns about herself and her own culture through her interactions with the Akans. Sutty's heroism is not characterised by physical strength or combat skills but by her determination, courage, and compassion. She is a hero because she stands up against an oppressive system and fights for what she believes is right. Sutty's actions are a reminder that heroes do not always have to be warriors or superheroes but can be ordinary people who stand up for their values and beliefs. Furthermore, Sutty's heroism is not individualistic but rather a collective effort. She recognises that the preservation of the Akans' cultural heritage is not just her responsibility but that of all those who value and appreciate the importance of cultural diversity. Her actions inspire others to join her cause, and she becomes a symbol of hope for those who are oppressed and marginalised. While Sutty's actions might be deemed as dangerous and even suicidal to a certain extent, by doing so, Sutty achieves what she was searching for—peace and reconciliation with her past.

Works Cited

Cadden, Mike. "Purposeful Movement Among People and Places: The sense of home in Ursula K. Le Guin's Fiction for Children and Adults." *Extrapolation*, vol. 41, no.4, 2000, pp. 338-350.

Cooper, Clare. "The House as Symbol of the Self." *The People, Place, and Space Reader*, edited by J.J. Gieseking, W Mangold et al., Routledge, 2014, pp. 168-172.

Cummins, Elizabeth. "The Land-Lady's Homebirth: Revisiting Ursula K. Le Guin's Worlds." *Science Fiction Studies*, vol. 17, no.2, 1990, pp. 153-166.

Dann, Graham M.S. "Anomie, ego-enhancement and tourism", *Annals of Tourism Research*, vol. 4 no. 4, 1977, pp. 184-94.

Garcia, Jeanette. *Deconstructing Domesticity and the Advent of a Heterotopia in Chuck Palahniuk's Lullaby*. Florida International U, 2012. *FIU Electronic Theses and Dissertations*, http://digitalcommons.fiu.edu/etd/581

Gurney, Craig. *Meanings of home and home ownership: Myths, Histories and Experiences*. University of Bristol, 1995.

Hendershot, Cyndy. "From Trauma to Paranoia: Nuclear Weapons, Science Fiction, and History." *Mosaic: An Interdisciplinary Critical Journal*, vol. 32, no. 4, 1999, pp. 73–90. *JSTOR*, http://www.jstor.org/stable/44029850.

Iso-Ahola, Seppo E. "Towards a social psychology of recreational travel". *Leisure Studies*, vol. 2, no.1, 2006, pp. 45-56.

Kotler, P and G.M. Armstrong. *Principles of Marketing*. Prentice Hall,2010.

Le Guin, Ursula K. "The Telling." *The Hainish Novels & Stories*, edited by Brian Attebery, The Library of America, vol. 2,2017, pp. 589-750.

Li, Wei and Dennis Tao Yang. "The Great Leap Forward: Anatomy of a Central Planning Disaster." *Journal of Political Economy*, vol. 113, no. 4, 2005, pp. 840–77. *JSTOR*, https://doi.org/10.1086/430804.

Lieberthal, Kenneth G. "Cultural Revolution". *Encyclopedia Britannica*, 5 Sep. 2023, https://www.britannica.com/event/Cultural-Revolution. Accessed 15 September 2023.

Murdock, Maureen. *The Heroine's Journey*. Shambhala, 2013.

Ning, Wang. "Introduction: Global Maoism and Cultural Revolutions in the Global Context." *Comparative Literature Studies*, vol. 52, no. 1, 2015, pp. 1–11. *JSTOR*, https://doi.org/10.5325/complitstudies.52.1.0001.

Smil, V. "China's great famine: 40 years later." *BMJ (Clinical research ed.)* vol. 319, no.7225, 1999, pp. 1619-1621. doi:10.1136/bmj.319.7225.1619

Spivack, Charlotte. *Ursula K. Le Guin.* Twayne Publishers, 1984.

Thrall, James H. "Learning to Listen, Listening to Learn: The Taoist Way in Ursula K. Le Guin's *The Telling.*" *Practicing science fiction: Critical essays on writing, reading and teaching the genre,* edited by Karen Hellekson, Craig B. Jacobsen et al. McFarland, 2014, pp. 197-212.

van Wee, Bert and Patricia Mokhtarian. "Escape theory: Explaining a negative motivation to travel." *Transportation research part A: policy and practice* 169 (2023): 103603.

Chapter 4

Carrying the Fire: *The Road* and Rituals of Resilience in a Dead World

Sakti Sekhar Dash

Social Science Research Council, Open Association of Research Society

Abstract

Cormac McCarthy's Pulitzer Prize-winning novel, *The Road,* paints a bleak and depressing picture of a post-apocalyptic world. In this world, which is merely a shell of its former self, a father-son duo makes its way across the barren wasteland trying to survive the "nuclear winter". Not only do they have to contend with the devastated landscape, devoid of vegetation, but also the gangs of cannibals prowling the roads. Where survival is of paramount importance, most of the survivors have abandoned the age-old morals and ethics, choosing to consume the flesh of other humans for sustenance. The man and the boy classify the people into "good guys" and "bad guys". While the so-called "bad guys" subscribe to an amoral and nihilistic form of existence, the "good guys" retain the values, ethics, and morals that have characterized the human world of the past. In a dead and desiccated world, these morals hold little meaning but continue to serve as a reminder of the past and the magnitude of loss incurred. Through seemingly insignificant little acts, the "good guys" re-enact the rituals that evoke memories of human civilization before the apocalyptic event took its toll. From these acts, the "good guys" draw the strength and resilience to survive, even when the odds are stacked against them. Wandering across the bleak and barren landscape of America, the father and his son continually remind each other that they are "carrying the fire" and will never stop being the "good guys". Thus, their wanderings are not confined to their physical resilience in the face of the inhospitable atmosphere and landscape but also test their moral fibre, which goes up against the lure of amoral nihilism when all vestiges of human civilization have fallen apart.

Keywords: Post-apocalyptic, Nihilism, Rituals, Ecology, Amoralism

***

Following in the footsteps of his literary predecessor, William Faulkner, Cormac McCarthy has emerged as the voice of the land. With works like *Blood Meridian*, *Child of God*, and *Outer Dark* he explored the darkest recesses of human consciousness. For the uninitiated reader, his works will come across as grotesque accounts of human depravity. But there is always an underlying sense of concern for the land and humanity beneath the veneer of violence and bloodshed. With the publication of *The Orchard Keeper* in 1965, Cormac McCarthy established himself as a writer of the American Southern tradition. For *The Orchard Keeper*, McCarthy won the William Faulkner Foundation Award. The work was a milestone in the canon of American Southern literature. Growing up in Knoxville, McCarthy experienced the nature and ecology of the American South from close quarters. *The Orchard Keeper* displays his sensitivity to ecology. The work also shows a deep-seated concern "for old and disappearing ways of life in the rural Tennessee hills" (Hage 8). McCarthy's emergence from the shadows of obscurity culminated in the publication of the Pulitzer Prize-winning novel *The Road*. As a consummate stylist employing figurative language, symbols, and allusions, McCarthy details the wanderings of a man and his son across the American landscape that is scarcely recognizable following a disastrous event. The sparseness of the prose adds to the sense of loss permeating the entirety of the novel. On the surface, *The Road* comes across as a novel recounting the final days of the human race. The tone of pessimism is difficult to miss. But for all the dark and depressing aspects of McCarthy's work, there is an underlying theme of hope and enterprise against insurmountable odds. The wanderings can be interpreted as a struggle for survival. Rather than wait for death to overtake them, the father-son duo journeys across the American South, hoping to evade the onset of the nuclear winter. The wandering is certainly not aimless. On the contrary, it carries a certain purpose and lends meaning to the otherwise hopeless nature of their existence. The novel features the recurrent motif of fire, which carries Promethean connotations. The Titan from Greek mythology refused to give up even in the face of the brutal punishment meted out to him for stealing the fire. He emerges as a figure of resilience and courage who stands by his belief. The father-son duo reiterates their faith in moral codes, which sets them apart from the "bad guys" and makes them one of the few "good guys".

Cormac McCarthy has never shied away from confronting the primordial tussle between good and evil. For the novelist, it has remained the greatest concern in human existence. The problem is compounded manifold when humans are confronted with different choices that could lead them along the paths of either good or evil. The characters in his novels frequently have to make choices that could define them as good or evil. Something similar unravels in *The Road* as well. The wanderings of the father-son duo serve as a metaphor; they have undertaken a journey where, at some juncture, they will be confronted with multiple choices. Their decisions will eventually decide their position as the "good guys" or "bad guys". But it is their moral compass that will decide the course of their journey. This essay proposes to understand the resilience and adherence to moral codes of the father-son duo in a post-apocalyptic world where chaos, lawlessness, and violence define human existence.

His novel, *The Road* can be best described as a meditation on human morality and meaning in human existence. The unrelenting gloom and pessimism of the narrative create a sense of eerie unfamiliarity and otherworldliness. The land is unrecognizable, and America is a thing of the past. All that exists in the present is a veritable limbo for doomed and tortured souls who make frantic efforts to survive in a world where death lurks at every corner. McCarthy drew upon his own experience to write the novel. When asked by Winfrey about what inspired *The Road*, McCarthy shared that he and his son John, to whom he dedicated the book, were staying in an El Paso hotel when the idea struck him. He stood by a window and heard the trains passing by with a haunting sound. He described having a vivid image of the post-apocalyptic landscape in his mind, envisioning fires burning on a distant hill (Hage 16).

He has deliberately chosen to leave most of the characters unnamed; this perfectly mirrors the post-apocalyptic land. Names are inconsequential when the known world is alien and hostile. The namelessness only adds to the sense of loss and vagueness of the present. Likewise, McCarthy is never explicit in mentioning the true nature of the catastrophe. "The clocks stopped at 1:17. A long shear of light and then a series of low concussions" (McCarthy 37). From this, it can be deduced that the event in question might have been a nuclear disaster. The catastrophe has triggered the demise of modern civilization. "The story is set in America, where all traces of modern society have stopped functioning. There is no electricity; there is no gasoline; there are no factories or stores or automobiles. Anarchy reigns in this desolate ash-covered world where the sun has been blotted from the sky" (Greenwood 77). Despite the setting being America, McCarthy hints at the possibility of the catastrophe engulfing the entire world. The father-son duo comes across a sailboat named Pajaro de Esperanza. The abandoned boat is from Tenerife, which indicates that the disaster may have spread as far as Africa. In this inhospitable American landscape that is hardly conducive for survival, a man and his son wander, foraging for food and looking for means to survive the cataclysmic event. The theme of wandering is a frequent occurrence in most of McCarthy's works. "Virtually all of Cormac McCarthy's fragmentary, often picaresque, novels are road or trail novels involving walking, riding, driving, rowing, or some combination thereof, and all of his characters are indeed *hombres del camino* or men of the road" (Josephs 133). The wanderings of the Man and the Boy are not devoid of purpose; they look to reach the warmer regions in the South. "It should be noted that this ashen world is the only one the child has known as he was born after the event itself, and the father's quest is largely motivated by his wish that his son will experience some of the life, culture, and civilization that he has never known" (Walsh 256). The mutual love and care between the father and his son is the sole shining light amidst the unrelenting gloom of the post-apocalyptic world.

The humans who survived the cataclysm must struggle against the elements and the hordes of cannibals. But most importantly, they must keep on moving. Failing to do so would invariably lead to their deaths either due to starvation or illness. "The ashen scabland infects everything, including pilgrim lungs, and walkers wear makeshift mouth scarves of torn sheets. The writing settles into a post-holocaust grammar of scree, shards, smoke, fractals, bits and pieces of charnel, dead flesh, and sallow bone" (Lincoln 165). The grimness of the narrative underscores the world that has emerged due to the human race's anthropocentrism. The relentless pursuit of anthropocentrism has pushed society to the brink of utter annihilation. The magnitude of devastation can be gauged from the description offered by McCarthy. Across the river valley, the roadway traversed a desolate, scorched area. Trees stood as charred, branchless remnants in all directions. Ash drifted over the road while the drooping wires hung from the burnt-out light poles emitted a faint whine in the breeze.[1] He conjures an image of desolation and death, which can be ascribed to the conflict between anthropocentric interests and the land. The conflict has resulted in a catastrophe that has destroyed all vestiges of human civilization. The environment appears desolate and reminiscent of a world after a catastrophic event.[2] Due to the catastrophe, most of the people have been killed; the few survivors struggle to live through a harsh winter. This has led to the creation of a new order that is brutal and barbaric. The strong prey on the weak. In order to endure, certain individuals have turned to consuming human flesh. Consequently, a fresh societal structure has emerged, dividing people into the survivors who strive to stay alive through scavenging and the predators who hunt other humans for sustenance. McCarthy presents an unsettling scenario for American society. Anthropocentric pursuits and relentless exploitation of the land and resources have led to the creation of a corpsed world where "Violent blood cults roam the landscape threatening to unleash all manner of unimaginable violence and break every possible taboo" (Walsh 257). In a none-too-cheery picture, "sojourners hold a plastic tarp against the sooty snow and rain of Puritan New England, pushing a shopping cart of scavenged provisions.

---

[1] Cormac McCarthy. *The Road.* (New York: Vintage, 2007): 6

[2] Willard P. Greenwood. *Reading Cormac McCarthy.* (California: Greenwood Press, 2009): 77

The golden-haired boy of possibly eight proves the father's "warrant" for living through end-times" (Lincoln 164). At the same time, they must stick to the codes that set them apart from the "bad guys". The code of principles followed by the "good guys" is a continuous reminder to remain committed to morality. Unlike the "bad guys", the "good guys" don't eat people, they don't steal, they don't lie, and they never give up. During the course of their wandering, the Man and the Boy frequently discuss these moral codes. While the Man struggles at times to remain a "good guy" in a world where morality is almost non-existent, the Boy renders him the strength and resolve to never give up on his principles. For the Man, the Boy is a constant reminder of God and his creation. Echoing the Book of Genesis, the Man considers the child to be his warrant to abide by moral principles. For him, the Boy stands as a testament to God's spoken word.

Apart from being a meditation on human morality *The Road* also voices McCarthy's concerns over the loss of faith in God and the values of the land. These can be ascribed to the rise of anthropocentric beliefs. The novel is a critique of the anthropocentric ways of the human race that are sure to sound the death knell of the land, ecology, and humanity. *The Road's* portrayal of America and the concerns shared by McCarthy has been aptly explained by Christopher J. Walsh. Similar to many distinguished American novels, *The Road* reevaluates the nation's connection to its land and geography. The catastrophe portrayed in the novel leads to descriptions of the landscape that resemble a collection of horrifying images, depicting a perpetual wasteland symbolizing an apocalyptic ecological awareness. This mirrors the evolution of the "wilderness aesthetic" identified by Guillemin in *Child of God*. Throughout the narrative, the landscape is described as "burned away," the terrain "cauterized," and the land itself is depicted as "gullied and eroded and barren." This includes references to a "jungle of dead kudzu," serving as a stark representation of the extent of devastation this invasive species cannot endure.[3]

It is not only a corpsed world but also one that is debased and evil. In a hauntingly lyrical passage, McCarthy projects the image of loss, decay, and death: "Dark of the invisible moon. The nights now only slightly less black. By day the banished sun circles the earth like a grieving mother with a lamp" (*The Road* 23). This lyricism is curiously reminiscent of the Book of Job. The horrors have obscured the goodness, and the barren American land is akin to a cold hell, with dead bodies impaled on stakes by the roadside.

The horrifying nature of the situation is amplified further by the cannibalistic acts practised by a group of survivors, which illustrate the destruction of moral codes and ethics. For their survival and interests, some people have resorted to

---

[3] Christopher J. Walsh. *In the Wake of the Sun: Navigating the Southern Works of Cormac McCarthy*. (Knoxville: Newfound Press, 2009): 266

killing and eating humans. Through their actions, they demonstrate their anthropocentric leanings. Anthropocentrism is based on the position of man as the only possessor of knowledge. Philosophers like Thomas Hobbes believed nature to be primitive, and it was the duty of man to subdue it. This promoted Utilitarian beliefs revolving around the general welfare of the community. For Hobbes, the comfort and safety of the human community were of utmost importance, and nature existed to fulfil human wants. Once the Theocentric tradition was rejected by Western thinkers, the relationship between God, Humans, and Nature was no longer accepted. Humans assumed the central position in the universe, replacing God and nature. Hobbes called for a scientific approach as a means to improve human existence. Judeo-Christian scriptures lamented the Fall of Man from the Garden of Eden. The Fall resulted in the loss of innocence and the alienation of Man from nature embodied by the Garden of Eden. The loss of Paradise and Eden has been perceived as the greatest loss on the part of the human race. Man lost the gift that had been presented by God. He was the guardian of Eden, but he committed transgression against nature. This is an example of an anthropocentric action on the part of Man. His disobedience of God's will reflects the changing position in the Universe. Previously, God had been at the centre of the creation along with the natural world with which he was closely associated. But Man's disobedience and transgression alienated him from God and nature, who were marginalized by humans. According to Thomas Hobbes, by consuming the fruit from the Tree of Knowledge, Adam and Eve gain the knowledge that had been withheld from them by God. By acquiring the knowledge of good and evil, they assume a central position in the creation (Hobbes 138). He believed that a scientific and rational approach could alleviate much of the suffering caused by the Fall. Before the Fall, Man enjoyed the bountiful abundance provided by God and nature. But after he is banished, he has to struggle and labour hard to eke out an existence. The generosity of God and nature has been replaced by his hard labour and enterprise. To survive and improve his condition, he has to employ scientific methods and rational thinking. Rational thinking questioned the position of God in the lives of humans while stressing obtaining comfort and security for the human community.

The beginnings of anthropocentric beliefs can be attributed to the writings of Lucretius. In his text, *On the Nature of Things*, Lucretius dismissed the idea of the divine's involvement in the world. He advocated for atomism, proposing that the universe consisted of material substances devoid of any divine intervention.[4] This outlook prompted the human community to regard non-

---

[4] Lucretius. *On the Nature of Things* "Book I". Cyril Bailey Trans. (Oxford: Clarendon Press, 1948): 45-53

human nature as 'matter'. Frederick Jackson Turner perceived the land as the property of the American settlers. It was a part of the Americans' destiny to tame and shape the land. By taming the wilderness of the West, the land could serve human purposes.[5] The Westward expansion meant the subjugation of the American ecology. It was a long and violent process through which the wilderness was conquered by the human community. This conquest coincided with the destruction of wildlife and indigenous communities, which were considered to be inferior when compared to the interests of the American settlers.

In *The Road*, the American landscape has undergone near-total annihilation. Human attempts to subjugate and exploit the land have eventually led to a catastrophe in which the human population has taken the biggest hit. The survivors' sojourn across the American landscape is nightmarish, to say the least. Cormac McCarthy's works are noted for the graphic depictions of violence, murder, infanticide, and necrophilia. But the nature of cannibalism presented by him in *The Road* is disconcerting. Humans are treated as food items stowed away in the pantry for consumption. The dehumanized treatment of human beings is the most disturbing aspect of the writing, and it highlights the loss of morality and faith. In a graphic description, McCarthy paints a gory picture of the horror witnessed by the Man and the Boy:

> Huddled against the back wall were naked people, male and female, all trying to hide, shielding their faces with their hands. On the mattress lay a man with his legs gone to the hip and the stumps of them blackened and burnt. The smell was hideous. (McCarthy 77)

The sheer objectivity of the scene adds to the sense of horror. There is scarcely anything human about the victims. They are sources of food for a group of people who have made a deliberate choice to abandon morality and embrace a nihilistic outlook. This scene, in particular, "emphasizes the futility of the father's quest to behave nobly in a debased world. He is surrounded by evil" (Greenwood 79). The cannibals subscribe to anthropocentrism. For their interests, they are willing to go to any extent, abandoning morality, faith, and God in the process. McCarthy makes it very clear that the days of an anthropocentric society are numbered. By promoting human interests at the expense of the land, the human community was creating a sense of alienation, which could only hasten the destruction of both the natural world and human society. The central idea forwarded through the post-apocalyptic novel is the destruction of the natural world. But the damage is irreversible. In the apocalyptic

---

[5] Frederick J. Turner. *The Frontier in American History*. (New York: Henry Holt and Company, 1921): 14-15

genre, the typical theme of the natural world rebounding to its former state without human intervention has been reversed. In *The Road's* conclusion, the natural order is beyond restoration. Human efforts to create a society based on an anthropocentric order have crumbled, giving way to chaos and anarchy in a corpsed world.

The ravaged world has been compared to a monstrous beast that is continually threatening to engulf the surviving humans. During a moment of rest, the Man has a vision. He sees himself being led by the Boy down stony passages that resemble the "inward parts of some granitic beast" (McCarthy 3). At the end of the stony winding passage, they come upon a cavern where lies an ancient lake. On the shore of the lake was a creature that was skeletal, blind, and soundless. The man sees the bowels, internal organs, and the brain preserved in a glass bell jar, pulsing feebly. This strange vision witnessed by the Man can be read as an allusion to the effects of anthropocentrism. The Boy, leading the Man, is a messianic figure, reminding the human race of the destruction wrought by anthropocentric pursuits. The creature is a symbol of primordial nature that has entered into a catatonic state. The alienation between humans and the natural world is complete and total. Nature has regressed to a primitive and savage form and stripped off the trappings of civilization, the humans have also regressed to a primitive state. The wasteland-like landscape offers little hope for survival, and the characters are always confronted by the fear of death. The fear of death has metamorphosed them into pilgrims seeking the sanctuary of the warmer South. Describing the belongings and the journey across the wasteland, Kenneth Lincoln writes:

> The things they might carry: a boy's toy truck, an incomplete pack of cards, a butane lighter, canned food of ham and beans, beets, carrots, anything that might not go bad, a nickel-plated pistol with two bullets, a plastic tarp and parka, decomposing shoes, binoculars, blanket rags, memories, hopes, courage, dreams, truth, a few words—all tumbled into a broken-wheeled shopping cart trundling down the road. (166)

The few possessions they carry with them are essential commodities and nostalgic reminders of the bygone days. The journey is a cruel and arduous one. The landscape also offers no solace to the eyes that might seek comfort in a tinge of green. The trees are dead and withered, signalling the death-like state that has gripped the land. "Everything paling away into the murk. The soft ash blowing in loose swirls over the blacktop. He studied what he could see. The segments of road down there among the dead trees" (*The Road* 4). Even the river is choked with ashes and is no longer flowing. Wherever the eyes rest, they are greeted by motionlessness, emptiness, and death. The image of stagnation and death is a foil to the wandering humans who are alive and on the move, even when the Man and the Boy stumble upon the comforts of an underground bunker provisioned with food, clothes, and bullets. Despite the tempting nature of the hideout, the father-son duo heads out on their quest after spending a few days in the cosiness of the bunker. The Man is well aware of the fact that sooner or later they will run out of provisions. With his health failing him, he knows that he is racing against time to reach safer regions.

The provisions the Man and the Boy find in the bunker serve as a temptation; they are confronted with the choice to continue on the journey or spend the rest of their time in the confines of the bunker. But the amenities that seem like a goldmine hold little meaning for the father-son duo who realizes that they are "carrying the fire" and must ensure it doesn't get extinguished. They have learned to live without the amenities that are closely tied to human comfort. Those very amenities are non-existent. It's a world dominated by nihilism; things like innocence, joy, and laughter are things of the past. There is an absence of humour, sorrow, verbosity, naivety, or reminiscing. Gone are the state roads, the concept of states altogether, border crossings, stores, vehicles of any sort, governments, laws, or ethical guidelines. Instead, there are only the putrid remnants of a decaying culture, violent gangs, corpses, and survivors sifting through the remnants of civilization, surrounded by the pervasive stench of decomposed bodies. The survivors have to exist without electricity and fuel, and the barren land cannot permit them to cultivate. The natural world no longer offers any warmth and comfort to humans. The sun barely provides any light where unremitting greyness meets the eye.

The degradation of nature has also coincided with the erosion of human ethics and moral values. The world has descended into chaos and anarchy as law and order have been cast aside. The survivors do not hesitate to kill one another and indulge in acts of cannibalism in the race for survival. In this brutally nihilistic world, the father-son duo preserves the vestiges of morality and conscience. They are the torchbearers of human goodness in an otherwise amoral world where evil is regarded indifferently. The journey they undertake is a quest to discover and come to terms with their goodness. It is also an opportunity for them to meet the few other "good guys" who preserve the last traces of goodness, morality, and humanity. In addition to self-preservation, they make every attempt to stay true to their roots and beliefs. Only by doing so can they stake claim to being the "good ones". There is a tussle between good and evil in a world where law, morality, and ethics have collapsed. In other words, nihilism rules large. The few who remember the past their moral codes have to contend with the "bad guys" who follow no morals. In this scenario, they prey on the good guys.

In *The Road's* nihilistic environment, meaning, morality, and faith in God have collapsed. The unnamed father-son duo makes its way across the blighted landscape, avoiding the "bad guys" and searching for food. Through their journey, Cormac McCarthy outlines the human capacity to endure hardship and suffering. But the resilience of the characters in the face of suffering is the shining light in an otherwise dark and gloomy narrative. The resilience stems from a belief in their conscience and a conviction that there are more "good guys" out there.

As a novelist, Cormac McCarthy viewed human relationships in an indifferent light. Dealing with the harsher concerns of human existence, he perceived traditional human relationships as insignificant. Whether it is the brother in *Outer Dark* or Suttree in the novel by the same name or The Kid in *Blood Meridian*, McCarthy's characters come across as doomed figures confronting the hard, cold, remote, and unforgiving truth about human existence before which common human relations appear pale and inconsequential. However, the filial love between the father and son emerges as the bright spot in the dreariness of the world where ashes rain down from the sky, and the sun stands blotted out. The ability to love and forge meaningful relationships with fellow humans aids them in their journey. It provides them with much-needed hope and faith to strive for survival and not succumb to the lure of evil. It is a perpetual struggle to survive "in a desolate world that appears to be deprived of moral order" (Hillier 263). But their ability to decipher good and evil while caring for their fellow humans lends meaning to their survival.

The only meaning present in the life of the Man is his unconditional love for his son. This encourages him to continue his struggle to survive and save his son in the bleak and inhospitable world. The sole connection anchoring him to this scarcely survivable existence is his son, born amidst the apocalypse and unfamiliar with any other reality. The Man's wife and the Boy's mother chose to end her life; she succumbed to despair and hopelessness. In the face of nihilism, she ended her life rather than continue with the struggle to survive abiding by moral principles. That is where the man differs; despite the bleakness of the situation and the scant hopes of making it through, he remains committed to his decision to carry "the fire". Till his last breath, he makes efforts to survive and remain firm to the moral codes.

The "bad guys" who are frequently spoken about in tones of terror represent the ultimate human depravity and nihilistic mindset. Human relationships, morals, and ideals like good and evil are inconsequential to them. On the other hand, the Man considers it his duty to save his child. He remarks, "My job is to take care of you. I was appointed to do that by God" (McCarthy 54). The divine directive has also imbued the father with a rigid moral code, a quality that seems out of place in a world lacking in humanity, order, and legal systems. While the "bad guys" are obsessed with destruction, the father and son try to preserve what they hold dear. In a scene that evokes nostalgia, the Man retrieves a can of Coca-Cola and hands it to the Boy. In the post-apocalyptic world, cans of Coca-Cola are literally non-existent. The Boy is filled with surprise to see the "bubbly" drink. In a heart-warming gesture of filial love, the Boy shares his can of Coca-Cola with his father:

> You have some, Papa.
> I want you to drink it.
> You have some. (McCarthy 16)

The Boy shows care for his father; it is a part of the moral code he has chosen to follow. They are Promethean figures, carrying the fire to keep the traces of humanity, morals, ethics, and values alive. Their choices can be contrasted with the decision made by the boy's mother. She resigns herself to her fate and refuses to struggle against the bleak circumstances. On the other hand, the Man and the Boy refuse to give up despite the odds being stacked against them. He has reposed his faith in a higher will, which fuels his struggle. As they traverse the terrain in search of sustenance, the father and son carry a collection of memories, aspirations, bravery, honesty, and a handful of words—all packed into a dilapidated shopping cart rolling along the pathway.

McCarthy paints a society that is severely divided and prone to violence. The division attests to the Cartesian influence as the society is structured into the "good guys" and the "bad guys". The "bad guys" are in control and the "good guys" have to struggle for survival. What separates the "good guys" from the "bad guys" is their refusal to give up their ethics and beliefs even in the worst crisis. The Man and his son are among the last surviving "good guys" who retain the ethics of the past. They can distinguish between good and evil, and this is the trait that sets them apart from the "bad guys" who are indifferent to ethics and morals. Cannibalism has remained a taboo throughout human history. By consuming human flesh, the people affirm their nihilistic character. The "bad guys" capture the "good guys" and consume their flesh. Even infants are not safe. In a scene that is shocking and disturbing, McCarthy details the roasting of an infant:

> They walked into the little clearing, the boy clutching his hand. They'd taken everything with them except whatever black thing was skewered over the coals. He was standing there checking the perimeter when the boy turned and buried his face against him. He looked quickly to see what had happened. What is it? He said. What is it? The boy shook his head. Oh, Papa, he said. He turned and looked again. What the boy had seen was a charred human infant headless and gutted and blackening on the spit. (McCarthy 139)

The "bad guys" are motivated by atomism and mechanistic thinking; they simply regard other humans as sources of food. Against the backdrop of complete societal and environmental breakdown, McCarthy delves into the essence and beginnings of the human drive to persevere despite overwhelming despair. The duo of the father and son represent the "good guys" who still remember ethics and morals. Despite the immensity of the odds, they stick together, and the father's love for his son compels him to protect him. The Boy and the Man still retain their consciousness regarding the ecology; the Boy shows his concern for the dog, which offers a spark of hope in an otherwise grim narrative.

In this moment of poignancy, the Boy and the Man show genuine concern for the non-human life forms. They share a similar fate, struggling to survive in a desolate land. Unlike the "bad guys" who prey on their fellow humans, the Man and the Boy still abide by the values and the ideals which are opposed to nihilistic thought. In *The Road*, McCarthy demonstrates the impermanence of human civilization. Human efforts to control the natural world through violent means only create turmoil, and the human race becomes the victim of its own actions. According to Christopher J. Walsh, "One of the recurrent themes throughout McCarthy's work is of our impermanence and irrelevance as individuals and as a species. His fiction repeatedly reveals the fragility of our attempts to control or order the world, and it frequently problematizes the supposed progress of our culture" (Walsh 261). In *The Road*, McCarthy presents one last conflict between the Cartesian forces and the ecological warriors. The latter are the marginalized characters in a world where social order has simply disintegrated.

Along with *Blood Meridian, The Road* is one of McCarthy's bleakest novels. *Blood Meridian* concludes with the murder of The Kid. *The Road* also ends on a similarly despairing note; the man dies, and the boy is taken in by a group of "good guys". But the final fate is never revealed. They inhabit an inhospitable world where the natural world has collapsed, and moral codes are non-existent. The novel ends on a note of uncertainty; the boy is one of the last "good guys", but the road ahead is rife with violence, nihilism, uncertainty, and death. But the Boy is "carrying the fire", signifying that he will continue the journey to preserve the ideals he has learned and ensure that God's message to the human race is never truly lost.

The wandering characters embody a curious kind of quest that is reminiscent of the search for the Holy Grail to restore fertility and order. But the quest that spans across days, months, and even years is a search for meaning in a desiccated world. "The power of The Road resides in the precise clarity with which McCarthy has rendered the destruction of the known world" (Greenwood 79). Despite the destruction of human civilization and the loss of human and ecological values, McCarthy does not ignore the overpowering presence of Cartesian influence. But the imminent destruction of the human race confirms the fact that human efforts to control the natural world, based on Cartesianism and atomism will not serve the human race in the long run. Lamenting the loss of balance and harmony, Fritjof Capra writes that the "sense of integrity and balance has been lost in our culture. The fragmented, mechanistic world view that has become all-pervasive, and the one-sided, sensate and "yang-oriented" value system that is the basis of this world view, have led to a profound cultural imbalance" (Capra 234). The man seeks to draw motivation from the long-lost ideals of the past. Time and again, he reiterates that they are "carrying the fire". This recurring motif denotes the sense of hope and optimism they preserve against all odds while wandering across the blighted American landscape. Simultaneously, they retain the age-old ethics and morals in an utterly nihilistic world, resisting the lure of violence and nihilism. Their resilience signals that all may not be lost.

Works Cited

Capra, Fritjof. *The Turning Point Science, Society and The Rising Culture*. Bantam Books, 1982.

Hage, Erik. Cormac McCarthy *A Literary Companion*. *Jefferson: McFarland & Company*, Inc, Publishers, 2010.

Hillier, Russel M. *Morality in Cormac McCarthy's Fiction: Souls at Hazard*. Providence: Palgrave Macmillan, 2017.

Hobbes, Thomas. *Leviathan*, New York: Oxford University Press, 1996.

Josephs, Allen. "The Quest for God in The Road". *The Cambridge Companion to Cormac McCarthy*. Ed. Steven Frye. New York: Cambridge University Press, 2013.

Lincoln, Kenneth. Cormac McCarthy *American Canticles*. New York: Palgrave Macmillan, 2009.

Lucretius. *On the Nature of Things*. Cyril Bailey Tr. Oxford: Clarendon Press, 1948.

McCarthy, Cormac. *The Road*. Picador, 2009.

Turner, Frederick J. *The Frontier in American History*. New York: Henry Holt and Company, 1921.

Walsh, Christopher J. *In the Wake of the Sun Navigating the Southern Works of Cormac McCarthy*. Knoxville: Newfound Press, 2009.

Further Reading

Alridge, John. W. "Cormac McCarthy's Bizarre Genius." Atlantic Monthly. Aug. 1994.

Angus, Ian. *Facing the Anthropocene*. Monthly Review Press, 2016.

Appignanesi, Richard ed. *Introducing Nietzsche*. Icon Books, 2005.

Ariew, Roger, Dennis Des Chene, Douglas M. Jesseph, et al. eds. *Historical Dictionary of Descartes and Cartesian Philosophy*. Rowman and Littlefield, 2015.

Ariew, Roger. *Descartes and the First Cartesians*. Oxford University Press, 2014.

Arnold, Edwin T. and Diane C. Luce eds. *Perspectives on Cormac McCarthy.* University Press of Mississippi, 1999.

Bell, Vereen M. *The Achievement of Cormac McCarthy.* Louisiana State University Press, 1988.

Bishop, Paul ed. *A Companion to Friedrich Nietzsche.* Camden House, 2012.

Bloom, Harold ed. *Bloom's Modern Critical Views Cormac McCarthy.* Infobase Publishing, 2009.

Boddice, Rob ed. *Anthropocentrism Humans, Animals, Environments.* Brill, 2011.

Crosby, Donald A. *The Specter of the Absurd Sources and Criticisms of Modern Nihilism.* Albany: State University of New York Press, 1988.

Davies, Jeremy. *The Birth of the Anthropocene.* California: University of California Press, 2016.

Hawkins, Ty. *Cormac McCarthy's Philosophy.* New York: Palgrave Macmillan, 2017.

Jarrett, Robert L. *Cormac McCarthy.* New York: Twayne Publishers, 1997.

Chapter 5

'Masi': The Wandering Subject in "Wake Up Call" in *Barbed Wire Fence* (2015)

Jabeen Yasmeen

IIT Bombay

Abstract

'Maasi ma,' i.e., aunt, yearns to go back to her home. Withered physically with age, with eyes that stare blankly at the person opposite her, Maasi ma has only one final destination in her mind: her motherland across the border. Her memory keeps on shifting, her identity is uncertain, and her dwellings are not fixed, yet this frail woman strives her best to go back to what she calls her long-lost home. In Amitabh Dev Choudhury's short story, "Wake Up Call" from the anthology Barbed Wire Fence (2015), Maasi ma's determination to go back to her home evokes in the narrator a multitude of questions of belonging and identifying with a land of one's own. This short story reflects on the meaning of documents and identity, the temporality of belonging to a space, and also, on the idea of being a refugee, especially in the context of Assam, where this story is located. On July 31, 2018, when the penultimate draft of the National Register of Citizens (NRC) was released, almost four million applicants were left out of the list, creating the largest potential cluster of stateless people in the world ever. Although this number came down significantly, the process of NRC and, later, the Citizenship Amendment Act 2019 evoked the angst of 'not-belonging.' This paper will try to read the fluidity of 'not belonging' through the wandering figure of Maasi ma.

Keywords: Border, Identity, Home, Memory, Space, Temporal Wandering

***

Introduction

"Come morning, the impatient knocks rain on the door," the narrator in "Wake up Call" tells us. The source of these incessant knockings on his door is the older woman in the neighbourhood, whom everyone calls Masi, aunt in

Bengali. Masi yearns to go back to her long-lost home. She is the ghost-like wandering subject whose ordeal amidst the necessity of documentation in the present-day nation-state of India is narrated to us by the narrator.

Masi is the protagonist in Amitav Dev Choudhury's short story, "Wake up Call" in the anthology *Barbed Wire Fence* (2015), translated from Bengali into English by Subha Prasad Nandi Majumdar. Similar to most of the other stories in the anthology, Masi's story also deals with the process and struggles of questioning, asserting, proving, and documenting one's identity. This anthology, edited by Nirmal Kanti Bhattacharjee and Dipendu Das, is a collection of stories, translated from Bengali, which are "negotiation[s] of the issues of displacement and marginalisation" (*Introduction* xii), especially from the Barak Valley of Assam. While the anthology also deals with the crisis of identity amongst the tea-tribe community-based in the Barak Valley, it chiefly engages with the angst of the Bengali population that migrated to the Valley during different waves of migration. Our protagonist in focus, Masi, seemingly belongs to the latter group. The narrator often tells us how Masi is an unreliable informant: her story has different versions very often, and her memory seems questionable. This shifting adherence to a definite stance contributes to making Masi what Achille Mbembe and R.H. Mitsch call the 'wandering subject'.

The "Introduction" to the anthology explains that the collection derives its name from the "barbed wire fence on the porous Indo-Bangladesh border," which, besides marking out the two countries geographically, also "stands as a wall between the peoples sharing a common culture, tradition and language" (ix). It further explains that "border-crossing, migration, and displacement" have become "the most important issues in the post-independence period in Eastern part of India, especially Assam" (ix). These issues have resulted in "displacement, the pang of being uprooted and crisis of identity" to be the thematic concerns of the Bengali literature of Assam for the first two decades after 1947 (xi). The exodus into Assam from the erstwhile East Bengal, later East Pakistan, and present-day Bangladesh was in different waves, one of the first and the largest waves being "after the referendum in Sylhet district on 6 and 7 July, 1947," wherein Sylhet was transferred to the Dominion of Pakistan. There were later waves of migration in 1965, "during Ayub Khan's regime" (x), i.e., the Indo-Pakistan War, and also in 1971, during the Bangladesh Liberation War (ibid.). The "Introduction" connotes that while the Bengali literature in Assam, immediately after 1947, focused on the pains of displacement and migration, the literature from the 1980s also began addressing the marginal existence and identity of the community that was a reaction to the emergence of the various identity assertion movements in Assam, chiefly the Assam Movement (1979-1985). As this process of identity-making continues in Assam, the stories in

Barbed Wire Fence are replete with these issues through translations of stories originally written in Bengali.

As this paper engages with the overarching question of identity in the story in focus, it reads the figure of Masi, the aunt, as a wandering subject. While the figure of Masi raises questions of belonging and not belonging, it also takes us to the process of documentation. This process of documentation is of great significance in a post-independence nation-state that is still caught up in a quagmire of identity formation. Leaning on Achille Mbembe and R.H. Mitsch's configuration of a wandering figure, I would argue that Masi also comes to embody the definition of what constitutes 'ghostliness.' Masi, as Mbembe and Mitsch theorise, lives on the edges and not the periphery. She is not an outcast; neither is she an active constituent and participant in the machinations of society. Her existence is negated and rendered redundant at times by the document-oriented, modern-day nation-state, and yet, she is resistant while she tries to navigate through the negation. As her worth can be determined only if she had 'proof' of her existence, could she also surpass the ghostliness? In her attempt to reach home, Masi is in a constant flow, from one village to another, inching towards the borders with all her physical and mental efforts. She becomes the 'wandering figure' in her struggle to stop being one. As Mbembe and Mitsch argue, "but there is no body except in and through movement. That is why there is no subject but a wandering one. The wandering subject moves from one place to another" (17). Although Masi seems to defeat the definition that wandering subjects do not need a "precise destination" (ibid.), her journey does not lead her to her "desired destination" since the role of the "unexpected and the unforeseen" definitely play their part in Masi's unwarranted journey. If only she can reach her homeland, which she constantly yearns for, will Masi stop being the 'wandering subject' that Mbembe and Mitsch define, yet ironically, her being a 'ghost' without papers spectacularly defeats her quest to home. This paper is a reading of all the attributes that qualify Masi as the 'wandering subject' and her strong-willed resistance to defy all odds that make her 'wandering subject': that she can "morph under any circumstances," i.e., resisting the processes of documentation as well as rejection by clandestine racketeers, and "going beyond oneself in an agonising, centripetal movement that is all the more terrifying as the possibility of returning to the centre is never assured" (Mbembe and Mitsch 19). This paper argues that this 'centre' that Masi tries to return to as the wandering subject is a temporal destination rather than a geographical one.

Masi and Homelands

As we already had a glimpse of it in the beginning, Masi would wake the narrator up early in the morning, even when the rest of the neighbourhood slept. Masi heeded no time or societal protocols in reaching out to the narrator and enquiring about the issue that seemed to be the sole purpose of her life now—to go back to her homeland. In the narrator's description of this protagonist, we cannot miss the gradual drawing up of a withered human figure: her hair is twisted like a rope, her face deeply wrinkled, "wilderness haunts her open eyes," a white cloth wrapped around her indicating her "bygone femininity," which otherwise would have been difficult to figure out (Choudhury 139). She is beyond any masculine or feminine attributes, she is "just Homo sapiens. Merely a human being" (ibid.). The physical depiction of Masi concludes with the assertion that she is a human being bereft of any gender attributes, while the description fleetingly hints at the "wilderness haunt[ing] her open eyes." This alone begins to imply Masi's non-belonging to any definite location. That she has surpassed her prime is explicitly pointed out. Her non-belonging to society is also highlighted in the fact that she is not restricted by the hour of the day when she decides to knock on the door of the irritated narrator.

Masi knocks on the narrator's door since he has promised to help her get back to her homeland across the border. Though the whole neighbourhood had come together to help Masi, a vagabond in the village, to live a frugal life of sustenance, she especially seeks out the narrator during such an early hour to enquire about the progress of the promise made. The narrator hints that there has not been much progress.

Masi's yearning for her homeland is accompanied by her ready storytelling of the past, especially of the place they are located in when the story is being told, which, in turn, gives a reason to the narrator to consider Masi as an unreliable narrator. Masi's narration of the place does not cohere with what the narrator has known as its history. The story, we are informed, is located in Silchar. Silchar is a city in Cachar district in the Barak Valley division of Assam.[1] Cachar district is one of the places that shares a border with present-day Bangladesh. The narrator points out, "Needless to mention, Masi can hardly be expected to be coherent in her narration. This story is basically cobbled in my imagination, in the confluence of Masi's disorderly dialogue and my acquaintance with the history of this town, Silchar of the British era" (Choudhury 140). Masi's stories create doubt in the narrator, who then tries to interconnect and verify if she indeed witnessed those events during the British era or if she had heard those stories from some secondary source (ibid.). Masi's stories become temporal overlaps: if she had witnessed the Silchar of 1936-37, how could she have

---

[1] The state of Assam is divided into three broad physiographical units: the Brahmaputra Valley in the north, the Central Hilly Regions of Karbi-Anglong and North Cachar, and the Barak Valley in the south (Government of Assam).

witnessed the East Bengal or Sylhet of the same time? The narrator further tries to figure out how Masi's stories work, wondering if "two different times live together in Masi's memory" or if "two different histories" have somehow connected in her imagination (ibid.). The narrator contemplates if living for too long has affected her memory, such that "what was her past has become her present" (ibid. 145). He lists the various discrepancies in Masi's narration of her life stories. She had once said that she was never married, which she later negated to say that she was married on the Indian side, again shifting to the other side of the border. Once, she also claimed that she had a son who now lives on the other side of the border. She would note that she had lost her mother during the partition, and yet at another time, she would narrate how all of them had crossed to this side of the country. And yet another totally different version of her story was how two persons had smuggled her and many others into this country to work as contractual labourers (ibid).

As the narrator introduces us to the uncertain temporal locations of Masi in the history of the city of Silchar, it becomes indicative that she seems to have a doubtful geographical origin as well as destination. One of the first glimpses into this uncertainty is when he told us how seven months ago, Masi came "drifting" into their locality without any belonging or destination to go to, and they, as a community, convinced the priest and the members of the committee of the temple to allow her to stay at the temple as well as make provision for her to eat there (ibid. 141). This uncertainty of belonging, as is emphasised in her 'drifting' to the narrator's neighbourhood, is challenged once Masi begins to assert her yearning to go back to her homeland across the border. She pleads, "For God's sake, please let me have a glimpse of my homeland. Once, at least. It keeps haunting me all the time" (142). She asserts that she is not drifting aimlessly but to her homeland.

Throughout the narrator's description of his encounters with Masi and her tireless longing to go home, we realise that she variedly lives up to Mbembe and Mitsch's definition of the "living dead" or "ghost." Masi lives in the periphery of society, not exactly on its edges, which Mbembe and Mitsch analyse as the lateral or ghostly space. It is this space where the "events continually take place that never seem to congeal to the point of consolidating history" (Mbembe and Mitsch 6). As Masi narrates her various experiences of the place of Silchar and the many ways that she has been a part of it, the narrator points out that there seems to be a possible gap between reality and her experience. Masi is in a space where "life unfolds in the manner of a spectacle, where past, present, and future seem to be interspersed" (7). As Masi tells the stories from her past, we realise that the reality of "before and after are abolished, while memory is destabilised" (ibid.). The wandering life that Masi seems to lead now is but a "life that is fractured and mutilated" (ibid.). Masi's narrations do not cohere with events and seemingly do not have verifiable origins. Some appear to be "pure-memory-filters" (ibid.).

As we are further told how Masi's prior attempt to return home was foiled, we realise again that she is qualified to be designated a 'living dead' or 'ghost' in varied ways. Masi's manner of living and risking arrest or even death resist the political impositions. As she seems to wander in that Silchar neighbourhood without any affiliation to historical location or political identity, her existence becomes what Mbembe and Mitsch would call "threshold or specular experiences" (1). She can be grouped under the human life that is subjected to conditions of life, which confer upon them the status of living dead or ghosts.

Masi becomes this ghost in many ways. While the term 'haunt' is used to describe the wilderness in her eyes and her experience of inner turmoil at the very beginning, her existence, described as a non-entity, is emphasised further when her attempt to cross the border is spectacularly thwarted. She is a 'non-entity' for both the countries "on either side of the barbed wire": the one she lives in now and the one she longs for as her home. The kingpin of the clandestine transportation racket denied her a passage without caring for her desperate pleadings, ignoring even the amount of money she was prepared to pay for the service. The narrator surmises that perhaps Masi is a 'non-entity' because she can "no longer deliver anything, either physically or mentally" (Choudhury 143). Even a fraudulent racketeer perhaps considered Masi "a rejected person," a person not valid enough to be duped, a person not legitimate enough to belong to worldly systems of human trafficking. Even the racketeer's rejection reveals Masi's existence as beyond the mainstream society and it's the threshold.[2]

Resistance and a Vortex of Documents

Masi's rejection as a person to be duped on the trip across the border makes her more determined to reach her home, and she resists submitting to the obstacles in her journey. On her return from this failed trip, Masi starts collecting torn papers and keeps them carefully in an old and rusty leather bag whose zip fastener doesn't even work. She collects especially those papers that have some resemblance to official documents. Needless to spell out louder, Masi assumed those torn papers to be her official documents to help her reach her homeland. It is only rhetorical when the narrator poses the question if Masi,

---

[2] However, when Masi disappears from the neighbourhood, the narrator finds that it was Masi's early morning knocks on his door that had kept his schedule in place. He overslept when Masi did not wake him up and his schedule was jeopardised for a few days. Thus, he hints that even a 'rejected person' had some implicit contribution to society.

"a rejected person," considers the heaps of waste paper to be her documents (Choudhury 144)?

Finally, one morning, Masi vanished from that neighbourhood in Silchar. As memories of this old woman gradually ebbed from the neighbourhood's daily conversations, the narrator saw her one night in Karimganj, where the river Kushiyara becomes the borderline between Indian and Bangladesh. As the narrator describes Masi haplessly, showing the piles of torn papers to the sentries, we witness what can be called the climax of Masi's ordeal and angst, as that of millions of others struggling in their daily lives to prove and claim a political identity.

> Masi stood there alone with her old, torn, black zip-less leather bag in hand, in front of sentries of the border post. I saw her showing the torn waste papers one by one to the stoic sentries. A rejected person exhibiting all the waste papers as her testimonials. These consisted of her passport and her visa to go across. Piles of waste papers, slipping out of her hand, cast a gloom over the entire surroundings. Soon, more and more waste papers started flying in from different directions to join their brethren. A huge avalanche of waste papers came down on the riverbank. A thunderstorm of waste papers enveloped the entire sky. Testimonials of a whole rejected population from all the places, who are bereft of any identity or lineage, are roaring along the riverbank. In this whirlpool of waste papers, their dreams and memories of a time lost are swirling. From thousands to millions, from millions to crores, they spiral incomprehensively. The incessant shower of rejected dreams and rejected memories is drowning the riverbank. The unending piles of waste papers have covered the riverbank in a numb white shroud (ibid.)

Masi becomes a representative of the "whole rejected population" regardless of their places and lineages. Being a 'rejected person', she comes to signify the arduous process of documentation that has become the crux of nation-making in a post-colonial nation such as India.

The process of documentation of a citizen in India has gone through many stages of change as the nation-state deliberated upon the idea of who is, and is not, and who can be, and cannot be, a citizen. Vazira Fazila Yacoobali Zamindar's work (2008) investigates this process of documentation of a citizen that India and Pakistan began to implement as both nations began witnessing challenges to the idea of nationhood and belonging. With the introduction of passports and visas, claiming citizenship became even more complicated in both India and Pakistan. From being a travel document, the passport shifted to a "certificate of citizenship, a means to establish state-bound national identity," and the different kinds of permits were replaced by visas, issued only for specific cities or towns, additionally requiring police reporting and/or registration at consulates (162). Zamindar depicts how the process of documentation had changed in the postcolonial states of India and Pakistan, bringing to the fore many cases of misplaced documents that had put an individual or a family's identity as rightful citizens into question. The process of acquiring a document, thus, becomes subject to the state's policies of acknowledging one as a rightful citizen. The process of being acknowledged by the state as a rightful citizen in India has incorporated newer complications in recent times through processes such as AADHAR enrolment,[3] the National Register of Citizens (NRC),[4] and the Citizenship Amendment Act 2019.[5] While these processes of enrolment involved intricate paperwork and awareness on the part of the citizens, they explicitly sounded out the significance of 'documents' in a nation-state such as India, today.

As these processes represent the grind and violence that is inherent in the processes of claiming citizenship, especially in a post-independence nation-state where the discourses and rules are still ambiguous and shifting, we can only imagine someone, such as Masi, being completely left out of them. We can perhaps also imagine that the turbulence of the political times could have inspired the creation of a wandering subject in literature, such as Masi. It is, thereby, that the narrator can envision the helplessness of "a whole rejected population" in the vortex of papers that are not documents. This vortex probably represented even those papers, which, despite being valid documents, fail to prove the belonging and citizenship of the one who furnishes them. The term 'paper' becomes an insufficient metonymy for documents: documents that prove one exists; documents that prove one's identity, including affiliation to a

---

[3] Aadhar (meaning foundation) is a "verifiable 12-digit number issued by UIDAI to the residents of India for free of cost" (UIDAI, Government of India). The Unique Identification Authority of India (UIDAI) is a statutory authority under the Aadhar Act 2016 by the Government of India. It was created to issue Unique Identification Numbers (UID), Aadhar, to all residents of India. It was believed that Aadhar is a proof of one's identity and thereby, one's citizenship, although the Supreme Court of India later rejected this claim. Assam and a few other states in the northeast of India did not have the mandatory enrolling for Aadhar till 2018.

[4] NRC was the process of updating the NRC of 1951. The Census documents of 1951 containing information on the relevant particulars of every person enumerated were copied in registers. Starting in 2013, citizens have to prove their family tree and their connection to a legacy data, a number that had been given during the NRC 1951 (Government of Assam, 2015). The final draft of the NRC released on August 31, 2019, left out almost 1.9 million applicants (*The Hindustan Times*).

[5] Citizenship Amendment Act, 2019, which "seeks to grant Indian Citizenship to persons belonging to Hindu, Sikh, Buddhist, Jain, Parsi and Christian communities on ground of religious persecution in Pakistan, Afghanistan and Bangladesh" (Government of India).

state, a nation-state, and a nation; documents that are evidence of belonging to a land that one can call home; documents that tell us of ownership of history and many other aspects that may prove that one does not belong beyond the threshold as a 'living dead.'

Wandering: Geographical or Temporal

As we begin to realise that Masi is the wandering subject living in the periphery, beyond the edges, and that she tries to resist her way through all the formalities that surpass her understanding, we also see her ironically evoking in the narrator the question of belonging and seeking a home. As the narrator describes the ordeal of Masi, he appears to have been located fixedly in that Silchar neighbourhood, generationally, in absolute opposition to the wandering subjectivity of Masi. Gradually, however, after Masi's constant nudging to help her go back to her homeland, he, too, begins to feel a yearning to go back to his roots. We are informed that the narrator's ancestors, too, had come from across the border at some point of historical upheaval. Although the narrator, himself, was born in Silchar, Masi's longings evoke in him a longing that has been passed through generations, which appear now as "imaginary sketches of my [his] homeland piled up over a long period of time in the sublime interiors of my [his] mind" (Choudhury 142). He begins to feel that Masi's homeland has become his homeland too, "the lost homeland which lurks beneath my consciousness for years" (ibid.). The narrator slowly unravels that even his mother, who had spent half her life on this side of the border, "used to yearn for her homeland" too (144), though she had lived "half of her life on this side of the border" (ibid.). This raises in him the question of why this land did not ever become his mother's homeland.

As we further listen to the emotional turmoil created in the narrator by Masi's constant nudging, we realise that the yearning to go back home is also a temporal wandering rather than a geographical dislocation. As he realises Masi's yearning is the same as that of his mother in her last days, he observes that it is, in reality, a yearning to go back to one's childhood and the memories associated with that childhood, "The search for one's homeland eventually becomes synonymous with the longing for one's childhood" (ibid.). Similar to Masi, as the narrator also yearns for a time that is past as did his mother, he, too, begins to identify as a rejected person for a fleeting moment. This angst of not belonging is also reflected in another short story in the same anthology, "Our Home" by Saumitra Baishya. In this story, too, the narrator's ancestors had migrated across the border in 1950. As the narrator's family settles in this new place, they grow as a family. The members move to different parts of the country, establish themselves as professionals, build newer homes in different cities of the new country, but simultaneously carry the rootlessness and yearning for home even after years. Towards the conclusion, the narrator confides in us, "My desperate attempts to gauge the depth to which the roots have gone inside went in vain every time" (Baishya 172). The roots of a past homeland and the roots of a present home are entwined, and there is no clear demarcation of how deep each of them can run inside us.

We are, then, confronted with different kinds of wandering that people carry in their beings, some as individuals and others as communities. Masi, as an individual, indicates multiple possibilities that must have caused her displacement and, thereby, wandering. The reason for the narrator's mother's displacement is also ambiguous: it could have been a political reason or due to the societal convention of being married away. In contrast, the narrator's own wandering represents that of a community generationally displaced from the land of their ancestors, which intensifies his own question of why a land does not become one's homeland even after spending half or all of one's life on it. The narrator's sense of displacement also stems from his being unable to relate to the technological changes that the times have brought and the paraphernalia of electronics that surround him. He constantly looks back to his childhood as a means of solace. It is a romantic yearning, where he reminiscences the "lantern-lit nights of fables and fairy tales," "the lush greens and thick of child-like adventures," or when he and his friends would escape the confines of closed classrooms to the freedom of playing a game of football or cricket to question if one can go back to the past or if a change of place can indeed make this possible (Choudhury 144-145).

The pining for a time past, especially one's childhood, is a longing for a safe, free, and loving space. The romanticisation of a past is a process of meaning making of one's location in the present. In her article, "Why Do We Romanticize the Past?" Charlotte Lieberman refers to Anne Wilson to explain that "we reconstruct what happened in the past on the basis of little bits and pieces of memory," which means that "the process of retrieving memories is 'highly reconstructive and prone to various biases.'" Lieberman informs that in 1994, two psychology researchers, Terence Mitchell and Leigh Thompson, called the phenomenon of biased reconstruction of the past "rosy retrospection," i.e., "recalling the past more fondly than we experienced it at the time." Rosy retrospection is, thereby, a process of navigating through the present with the comfort of memories pulled up from the past. Thus, the narrators in "Wake up Call" and also "Our Home," along with our protagonist, Masi, reiterate together that it is not exactly a geographical or spatial displacement that converts them into wandering subjects but rather a displacement in time. This is enunciated by the narrator when he arrives at the understanding, "What Masi is searching for is essentially a magic key that can take her back to her past. But the time that she is obsessing over, has withered away from the face of this planet long ago" (145). Thus, Masi's wandering subjectivity may have arisen out of nostalgia for a time long lost. Her journey would continue even if she succeeded in crossing to the other side of the border. Her homeland may forever elude her.

Conclusion

Masi remains the quintessential wandering subject with resilience: she singlehandedly resists the constraints that prevent her from reaching out to what she imagines to be her homeland. She dedicatedly pursues the processes that could offer her the possibility of achieving her lone goal. Even as she collects waste papers and tries to figure out ways to reach her homeland, she may not even remember exactly when she came, who she was, or her family both before and after marriage; however, she remembers the destination she has decided for herself. This wandering subject wants to reach a "permanent shelter"; that is why she resists the obstacles and "which is why she wants to be on the move further" (Chowdhury 146). Masi is the wandering subject that resists the strictures of society despite being on the edges and wanders from one place to another. She defies the limitations of being in the in-between spaces as a 'living dead,' trying to reach her home. Masi tries to navigate through the lateral sphere only to end up representing all those who seem to inhabit the same political, lateral sphere that she is herself in without the 'papers' of valid identity. As she evokes in the narrator a sense of being displaced, not just geographically but temporally, Masi reiterates that she may forever be the wandering subject in search of her lost home.

Works Cited

"About UIDAI." *Unique Identification Authority of India, Government of India,* 25 April 2023, https://uidai.gov.in/en/about-uidai/unique-identification-authority-of-india.html.

Baishya, Saumitra. "Our Home." *Barbed Wire Fence,* edited by Nirmal Kanti Bhattacharjee and Dipendu Das, Niyogi Books, 2015, 160—172.

Bhattacharjee, Nirmal K., and Depend Das, editors. *Barbed Wire Fence.* Niyogi Books, 2015.

Choudhury, Amitabha D. "Wake Up Call." *Barbed Wire Fence,* edited by Nirmal Kanti Bhattacharjee and Dipendu Das, Niyogi Books, 2015, 139—148.

"Complete NRC Draft." *Government of Assam, Home and Political.*18 April 2023, https://homeandpolitical.assam.gov.in/resource/complete-nrc-draft.

Lieberman, Charlotte. "Why Do We Romanticise the Past?" *The New York Times,* 2 April 2021, https://www.nytimes.com/2021/04/02/smarter-living/why-we-romanticize-the-past.html. Accessed 18 March 2023.

Mbembe, Achille and R. H. Mitsch. "Life, Sovereignty, and Terror in the Fiction of Amos Tutuola." *Research in African Literatures,* vol. 34, no. 4, 2003, http://www.jstor.org/stable/4618325. Accessed 01 November 2015.

Parashar, Utpal. "Over 19 Lakh Excluded, 3.1 Crore Included in Assam NRC Final List." *Hindustan Times*, 24 June 2020, https://www.hindustantimes.com/india-news/assam-nrc-1-9-million-names-excluded-from-final-list/story-KOlZwevNzXlKgrhpbDZvlO.html. Accessed 15 March 2023.

"Parliament Passes the Citizenship(Amendment) Bill 2019." *Press Information Bureau, Government of India, Ministry of Home Affairs*, 11 Dec. 2019, https://pib.gov.in/newsite/PrintRelease.aspx?relid=195783.

"The State Magazine." *Government of Assam, Mines & Minerals, Directorate of Geology and Mining*. 20 May 2023, https://dgm.assam.gov.in/frontimpotent data/the-state-magazine.

Zamindar, Vazira Fazila Yacoobali. T*he Long Partition and The Making of Modern South-Asia: Refugees, Boundaries, Histories*. New Delhi, Penguin-Viking, 2008.

Chapter 6

Construction of Maternal/ Womb Space and Her-Story in Andrea Levy's *Small Island*

Ijeoma Odoh

Princeton University

Abstract

Central to Andrea Levy's *Small Island* is the mass migration of members of British former colonies to Britain in the postwar era and their contributions to the redefinition of British society and national identities. The journeys (both physical and psychological) that former members of British colonies embarked on at this historical moment speak not only of their search for an alternative self-identity and economic improvement but also of their resilience and quest for inclusion in spaces and places where they have been displaced. Conversely, these journeys cut across geographic, gender, and historical boundaries as each of the characters repositions and seeks alternative spaces of being having been displaced by the war. Exploring their resilience and determination to survive through Deleuze and Guattari's concept of the rhizome or what I have reappropriated and referred to as rhizomatic womb-space theory—I seek not only to explore these moments of displacements but also to compare the female migrants/ the wandering subjects to the rhizome, which when broken or injured in one location, emerges elsewhere with multiple openings and growths. I argue that, like the wandering womb, which resists fixity as it searches for new pathways, women who migrate reconstruct their identities through routes and various connections and contacts they make rather than through roots. In situating characters in a rhizomatic womb-space, therefore, what is important is not race, class, gender, or nationality but making connections, giving voice to the voiceless, redefining women's social positioning, and fostering new social relations geared towards creating a conducive environment for people as well as breaking not just one new ground but multiple ones as people begin to question and critique the binary oppositions that set them apart, create new spaces for minority voices to be heard and for minority stories to be retold.

Keywords: Black British women, Identity Reconstruction, Migration, Rhizomatic Womb-Space, Wandering Womb

***

Introduction

Andrea Levy has been referred to as the "child of the Empire" as she was born a few years after her father migrated to England on board the Empire Windrush. Born in London on March 7, 1956, Levy has continually laid claim to British national identity. Like Caryl Philips, she is considered part of "a generation of writers who were born in Britain, educated in Britain and [who] because of their heritage and parentage, [have a] 'take' on Britain [that] is viewed through different glasses from those born elsewhere" (Sesay, qtd. in Perfect 31). In an interview with the Guardian entitled, "This is my England," Levy declares, "I am English. Born and bred, as the saying goes... and not born-and-bred-with-a-very-long-line-of-white-ancestors-directly-descended-from Anglo Saxon. English is my birthright. England is my home. An eccentric place where sometimes I love being English" (n.pg). Thus, in all her novels, questions of identity, (un)belonging, nationality, and dislocation are raised. In telling these stories, Levy draws the attention of her readers to the struggles and challenges immigrants face in their bid to understand who they are and where they belong. For her, identity is an enigma because many immigrants still do not understand their identities as they straddle two or more cultures. Even after declaring Englishness as her birthright and England her home, Levy shows how challenging these issues can be when she asks in that interview with the Guardian, "Identity! Sometimes it makes my head hurt—sometimes my heart. So, what am I? Where do I fit into Britain, 2000 and beyond?" (n.pg).

Levy's difficulty in defining her identity in Britain stems from her personal experiences in London as well as those of her parents. As Levy notes in that same interview with the Guardian, when her parents migrated to England in 1948, they not only had a problem finding proper accommodation but also found it difficult to be gainfully employed. Her father, though a bookkeeper in Jamaica, could only work for the post office and her mother, a trained teacher in Jamaica, had to sew to make a living in London while she re-trained as a teacher. As a growing child, Levy said she did not know much about her Jamaican identity. Before a racial awareness workshop, where other participants classified her as Black, Levy thought she had no other identity other than English identity. She explains to Gary Younge in an interview that her indifference to black racial identity was a result of her misconception of black people. As she states, "I thought black people were doing something else that I wasn't a part of. I felt embarrassed to go to their side. Not ashamed. I just thought, 'I don't know anything about being black'" (n.pg). However, her experience at the racial awareness workshop marked a turn for Levy, who then became interested in Black history and culture. Thus, in many ways, she uses her creative writing to explore and express the experiences and history of black people. As Michael Perfect notes, Levy's fiction explores the "silences and the unspoken" histories and experiences of black people at different historical and cultural moments (32).

Levy begins her story in *Small Island* with a prologue that speaks of the gathering of colonial subjects at the British Empire Exhibition that took place in Wembley in 1924. Although the colonial subjects are portrayed as uncivilized, the Exhibition sets the stage for alterity in social relations and in the rewriting of history that renders the former members of British colonies invisible through an encounter between an African man and Queenie—portrayed as the archetypal figure of England, the Mother Country. By offering to shake hands with Queenie rather than be seen and treated as a savage and a second-class citizen as many colonial subjects were treated during this historic moment, the African man not only changes Queenie's perception of Africa (portrayed in the novel as a jungle, where people are not civilized, sit on a dirt floor, wander, and get lost) but also speaks himself into subjectivity. The quest to reposition oneself becomes a leitmotif in the narrative as events and human contacts offer new perspectives for both Blacks and Whites[1] to reconstruct their identities. Significant is the fact that black women are at the forefront of this colonization mission[2] as they take

---

[1] The term "Black" in this paper refers broadly to people of colour and the term "White" is used to designate British Caucasians.

[2] The term "colonization in reverse" refers to the quest by former members of British colonies not just to take back what belongs to them but also to settle down in England and to have a prominent voice in the post-war British polity. In this paper, it is used as a metaphor to portray the resilient acts of immigrants to claim their rightful place in England. As Levy explains, Britain benefited both economically and culturally from its long stay in the colonies. They not only took from the colonies their natural resources but also used same to develop their countries, leaving these colonies impoverished. Thus, just as many white Britons benefitted from the wealth garnered from these colonies without working for it, some of these immigrants were looking forward to enjoying the "abundant wealth" in England they believe they are entitled to. Thus, aware of their subjugation during the colonial era and their poor economic conditions, it is their intention not only to get a job and settle down in England but also to rewrite the history that portrays them as inferior beings, renders them invisible, and erases their subjectivity.

The term is also associated with Louise Bennet's poem, "Colonization in Reverse" where she portrays the impact of post-war migration on Britain as well as the desires of immigrants to reposition themselves. In her poem "Colonization in Reverse," Louise Bennet describes post war migration as an act of colonization in reverse, as she details immigrants' determination to build a home and settle down in England. Responding to Louise Bennet's poem, Ashley Dawson contends that, "migration to the metropolis is not

up the responsibility of nurturing a new British multicultural society and fostering new social relations, as the character Hortense does in the novel. Hortense's ability to reposition herself socially and historically paves the way for her to construct what I have termed her 'rhizomatic womb-space'—a social, creative, ideological, and biological space through which women conceive, nurture, and offer new social relations built not on the either/or dichotomy that gender, class, race, and nationality evoke but on fluid identity formations and social relations. She not only becomes the voice that opens and ends this important narrative but also is the lone voice that speaks of the birth and nurturing of a new British multicultural society. Her advocacy for the recognition and inclusion of black women's distinctive experiences and perspectives makes a case for thin multiculturalism. Andrea T. Baumeister defines thin multiculturalism as a form of diversity where notions of difference and particularity are promoted and not relegated to the background. According to her:

> Thin multiculturalism refers to instances of diversity where the various
> protagonists continue to subscribe to a shared set of liberal values. While
> the advocates of thin multiculturalism stress the political significance of

---

a footloose escape from the parochialism of the islands for Bennett. Her poem implicitly suggests that this migration is also a willful and aggressive act, one that springs from the bloodstained history of colonialism and slavery in the Caribbean" (3). In other words, in view of the social imbalance and inequality that characterized the relationship between the Empire and its colonial subjects, Bennett contends that instead of unequal distribution of wealth and power crippling these colonial subjects, they have been emboldened to question their social positioning and subjugation. Like the colonial masters who brought their languages, religions, and cultures to bear in the colonies during the colonial period, these immigrants are turning history upside down as they make visible their languages, cultures, and religions in their new diasporic environments amidst opposition to their arrival and discrimination against them. As the poem's speaker in Bennett's poem expresses, "Jamaica people colonizing Englan in reverse/ by de hundred, by de t'ousan/ from country and from town…Dem a-pour out o' Jamaica, everybody future plan/ is fe get a big-time job/ an settle in de mother lan…an tun history upside dung" (qtd. in Dawson 3-4). Although Levy acknowledges the initial challenges that these immigrants face on arriving in England, she also notes the progress they have made in claiming their rightful positions in England. As the speaker notes, while some of the immigrants would settle down to work, some will settle for the "dole" or welfare package by so doing taking back from England the money they siphoned from the colonies through exploitation and exportation of their natural resources. By colonizing England in reverse, therefore, these immigrants are able to reposition themselves and write themselves back into history as they are actively engaged in redefining and rewriting British history and cultural identities.

.

group membership and as such reject the notion that difference and particularity should be relegated to the private sphere, they nonetheless endorse the liberal vision of individual rights and freedoms, including core liberal values such as individual autonomy and the equality of moral worth of all persons. Advocates of thin multiculturalism tend to see group membership as a key aspect of individual identity and, consequently, regard the recognition of cultural and social differences as vital if all individuals are to be guaranteed a secure environment in which they can flourish. Thus, for example, the debate between French and English-speaking Canadians or the demands by feminists for the recognition of women's distinctive experiences and perspectives are best seen as instances of thin multiculturalism. (36)

As she further notes, the two pivotal concerns of thin multiculturalism are the protection of minority cultures and effective political participation (76). However, unlike thin multiculturalism, advocates of thick multiculturalism think that their values and aspirations conflict with the wider liberal framework, especially when they feel that exposure to such values will undermine their commitment to their cultural and individual values. As an advocate of inclusion and recognition of people's distinctive cultural values, Hortense does not fear that her black cultural values should be in conflict with the dominant British culture or that her exposure to the dominant culture will undermine her cultural values as she knows that her culture is not inferior to the British culture and uses every opportunity to showcase her culture and to draw Queenie's attention to this rich culture, which has been neglected in the dominant British history. Thus, through her constant questioning of British homogenous culture and superiority and juxtaposition of her Jamaican culture and tradition with the dominant British culture, Hortense makes a case for its inclusion in British history and cultural values. As Stuart Hall contends, "there is no English history without that other history" (49).

Undergirding Levy's narrative is, therefore, a journey of self-discovery and recovery for both white and black protagonists. The novel captures Blacks' experiences in Britain before and after World War II. The story, which is told by four different first-person narrators—Gilbert and Hortense (a black couple), Bernard and Queenie (a white couple)—depicts the different journeys each of these characters must undertake to reconstruct their own identities and the different histories that shape those identities. The story is broadly divided into two temporal moments represented as 'Before' and '1948'—and each of these moments reveals the tensions and changes that shape both their personal histories and the national ones. While the 'Before' moments speak of events that took place before the post-war mass migration to England (in Jamaica, London, and the lives of these different characters), '1948' speaks of the arrival of the immigrants in London or what is generally referred to as the *Empire Windrush*[3] and the changes that come as a result of their arrival.

While most of the events take place in London, Levy interweaves these events with other ones taking place in different locales in her bid to defy a singular story and to deconstruct the myth of British homogeneous identity. She does this by allowing each of the characters to speak, each interpreting history and events as they impact his/her life. Thus, through multiple narratives and histories, Levy explores the impact of colonialism, slavery, and migration in the restructuring of British society. Conversely, the journeys upon which the characters embark, both physical and mental, cut across geographic, gender, and historical boundaries. There are movements to Jamaica, India, America and even within London. There are voices of men and women intersecting as they share their individual and collective stories.

Migration becomes a powerful movement that allows social repositioning and fostering of new social relations. For Blacks, especially, who have been subjected to different forms of displacements and exclusions from British nation and history, post-war II migration is portrayed as a wilful and aggressive act geared towards claiming their legitimate rights and place as British citizens. As Levy explains in an interview with Tracey Walters, Britain benefited both economically and culturally from its long stay in the colonies. They took from the colonies their natural resources and used same to develop themselves, leaving these colonies impoverished. Thus, similar to the long presence of the Europeans in the colonies that dispossessed people of their land, language, and culture, these immigrants are moving to England *en masse* to benefit from the wealth stolen from them as well as to have a stake in the British national polity. In this vein, this paper argues for the reading of post-war migration as colonization in reverse, as Blacks not only demand their rightful positions in post-war Britain but are also actively engaged in redefining and rewriting British history and cultural identities. In this regard, colonization in reverse becomes a metaphor that portrays the resilient acts of immigrants to claim their rightful place in England.

Literature

Critical studies on *Small Island* revolve broadly around race, identity issues, questions of (un)belonging, the building of a diaspora community, the politics of space and place and the application of rhizomatic womb-space theory on the text. Scholars such as Alicia Ellis, Corrinne Duboin, Thomas Bonnici, and

---

[3] *Empire Windrush* refers to mass migration of about 492 Jamaicans to England on June 22, 1948. It derives its name from the ship, "My Empire Windrush" that conveyed this first-generation of Jamaican immigrants.

Kim Evelyn pay particular attention to both pre-war history portrayed in the prologue and post-war history. While Kim Evelyn and Thomas Bonnici, who focus on post-war history, make a case for the various ways through which Levy deconstructs the historical narrative of Britain to create an alternative history of a hybrid, multi-ethnic, and multiracial British society, Alicia Ellis and Corrinne Duboin, who focus on the prehistory argue that the creation of British multiculturalism begins not in the post-war period but before the war. For Ellis and Duboin, the British Empire Exhibition of 1924 provides another singular moment through which the peripheral Other is incorporated into the centre.

Alicia Ellis contends that rather than the *Windrush* migration, the 1924 Exhibition represented in the novel's prologue marks the beginning of a multiracial British society. According to her, the prologue foregrounds many of the novel's central concerns about race, libidinal impulses, and language. She further notes that Queenie's cultural identity and nationalistic views are reshaped through her imagined encounter with Africa and her actual encounter with an African man. These encounters frame her subjectivity and identity and influence how Queenie interprets difference as an adult. According to Ellis, the prologue "sets the stage for the subversion of realism throughout the novel by showing that the so-called realities of history are underpinned by pre-existing colonial discourses, myths, misnomers, and fictions of identity" (76). On the other hand, Corinne Duboin argues that "[t]he exhibition draws a new cartography of Britain's hegemonic expansionism" (4). For Duboin, the "coming of the colonized to metropolitan space is a symbolic return to the womb, an invagination that does not simply allow the colonial encounter with the Other" (4). Although the return to the womb that Duboin evokes implies a double colonization, she later notes that the Exhibition sets the stage for alterity. In other words, the Exhibition sets the stage for colonization in reverse.

Other scholars who focus on post-war history see that history as the creation of a multicultural, multiethnic, and diasporic home in England. Focusing on the challenges Blacks in the post-war period faced, ranging from Blacks' unrecognizability of mother country, British's rejection of Blacks through repressive immigration laws, denial of housing and job opportunities, and racism, Kim Evelyn notes not only how "migrants had to come to terms with the idea of London as an illusion, as a dream built on the foundations of the colonial myths" (131) but most importantly, how "the domestic spaces…become spaces of promise and security as characters fight to claim them, keep them, and use them as diasporic hub where they can maintain dignity in the face of discrimination" (131). Unlike the minor and subordinated roles women play in the novels of the Windrush generation, especially in Sam Selvon's *The Lonely Londoners,* where women are portrayed as sexual conquests and silenced, Evelyn notes that black women's roles and social positions are transformed in

Small Island. According to her, "Not only are Levy's diasporans, like Selvon's, gathering in degraded housing to discuss their experiences and bonding their diasporic connections, but her work is also much more heavily invested in the improvement of living conditions as both refuge and freedom.... [these women] become equally invested in resistance to the racist oppression experienced outside of the home" (13). In terms of characterization, she notes that Black women are fully formed complex primary characters whose homemaking becomes a site of resistance as questions of nation and belonging are contested and (re)negotiated in the home space. Bonnici also focuses on the making of home in Britain for the Jamaican diasporic subjects, Hortense and Gilbert. He explains that although these immigrants are invited to the Mother Country, their inability to find suitable accommodation makes life challenging for them. Bonnici notes that it is only when they settle down as diasporic people that they realize that the Mother Country is neither a mother nor a home. He contends that the racist treatments that these immigrants face lead one to question the location of the home in the diaspora. According to him, Britain will never become a home for them because they are "thoroughly racialized in Britain and excluded from British society by every metropolitan native" (95). For Bonnici, home "is imagined to be a mythical place of desire which, characteristic of the diaspora, has to be constructed through experience" (95). However, I contend that if a home is established through people's experiences, the novel reveals that nobody, including native British citizens, is satisfied with either his/her experiences before the Empire Windrush and in 1948, hence the renegotiation of identities. This is because the many years of slavery, colonialism, and the war altered their lives in different ways. For the Jamaican immigrants, the many years of subjugation and exploitation by the colonial masters compel them to leave their country of birth to settle in Britain. For Bernard and Queenie (white British citizens), the war experiences bring them to their knees as they have to renegotiate their identities. For instance, Queenie has to go on her knees to beg both Hortense and Gilbert (a black couple) to take her biracial child. Bernard, on the other hand, feels alienated when he returns from India as a result of the devastation that occurred during the war, as well as the presence of immigrants in a country he once conceived as homogenous. As Ellis notes, "all the characters undergo experiences of displacement and re-settlement, all become migrants and refugees in different ways as they face the need for small islands to communicate or connect, and as England itself is displaced and unsettled" (263).

For Whites and Blacks, therefore, there is a need for identity renegotiations. For the immigrants, both World War II and post-war migration offer them the opportunity to reposition themselves, moving from their marginal positions to the centre as well as finding a voice to speak. Similarly, the war offered them the opportunity to begin to practically lay claim to British national identity as they fought alongside their white counterparts. For white Britons, they are forced to face the reality of the waning glory of England and its eventual demise as a superpower. As Irene Pérez Fernández contends, the post-war period signals "a moment of social disruption and change [as] all characters are forced to renegotiate their sense of identity and space" (150). In this regard, "Hortense and Gilbert have to (re)imagine the notion of the Mother Country and (re)negotiate a new reality after migration; Queenie has to go through the war on her own and is forced by social circumstances to give away her black boy; Bernard is obliged to dismantle his whole system of beliefs and accept the presence of black citizens in London" (150).

Although these scholars have explored the various themes in the text (racism, (un)belonging, disillusionment, displacement, homelessness, and prejudice) through the different histories that Levy portrays in the novel, it is the position of Queenie's biracial child in British society, the World War II history that produces him, and the roles of black British women in the construction of British multicultural society that has not attracted a great deal of critical attention. The few scholars who have explored World War II history and the position of the biracial child have done so in a fleeting manner. For instance, Sofia Munoz-Valdivieso sees the war as "a necessary reminder that before the Caribbean workers came to reconstruct the country in 1948, they have participated in the war effort, mobilized by their allegiance to what they deeply felt was their 'Mother Country'" (162). While it is true that the war is a constant reminder of the participation of members of former British colonies to reconstruct the country, it is equally true that the war not only brought black men and white women into intimate relationships but also produced biracial children. Similarly, just as World War II history has been touched upon slightly, many scholars do not see Queenie's biracial child as having a place of his own in the British social milieu. Michael Perfect contends that in giving away the child, "Levy not only suggests that the Britain of 1948 is 'not ready' but implicitly asks whether contemporary Britain is" (39). Similarly, Bonnici argues that Queenie's biracial native child "will never be at home in his own country. His only home will be the home of a diasporic black couple rejected since the very moment they set foot in the country" (97). John McLeod compares the child to Galahad's enigmatic and forgotten child in Sam Selvon's *The Lonely Londoners*. Relating the fate of Queenie's biracial child to the racial prejudice that Selvon portrays in his novel, McLeod not only contends that "the best place for a child who looks black is with a black family" but also suppresses and neutralizes the child's individuality" (50). Contrary to these arguments, this paper contends that both the presence of a biracial child and World War II history is significant in the overall construction and understanding of the other stories and histories in the novel. As the novel reveals, it is during the war that many of the transformations in British society begin to take place, especially in terms of the redefinition of British national identity, as well as immigrants becoming an integral part of British society as they are granted British citizenship. It is also during the war that black soldiers, represented by Gilbert, question their second-class position and also react against that position. Similarly, although Queenie's biracial child is produced during the post-war period, the foundation of this new birth is laid during the war when Queenie first meets Michael and engages in a sexual relationship with him. Thus, in addition to the dismantling of the Empire, World War II marks the beginning of a new multicultural British society.

Similarly, oftentimes, migration is usually explored through the lens of homelessness and displacement but not so much on emplacement, especially for women who most often are displaced from their roots. As such, little or nothing is said about how access to mobility helps female migrants reconstruct their identities and rewrite history. In this regard, this paper also focuses on the impact of migration on immigrants, especially black female migrants and how migration helps to reposition them and to emplace them in places they have been displaced, especially about their ability to rewrite history, break their silence and create a diasporic space that allows multiple voices to speak and multiple stories to be retold. It is significant to note that the various journeys embarked on by these characters bring to bear new social relations as their social orientation changes through their encounter with members of the British community, represented by Queenie and Bernard. However, while migration does not transform Bernard so much or help change his agelong opinion about the domineering power of the British Empire and his view about former members of the British colonies remaining in their historical places because of his sense of entitlement and privileged position as a white Briton, for the marginalized Black community, migration is conceived as an act of resistance and resilience, especially in ways in which it helps them to question their displacement and seek to emplace themselves in the British national polity and culture. Although each character is indeed displaced in one way or the other through the psychological and physical journeys they embark on, migration provides them with the opportunity to discover something new about themselves and others, as well as a chance to reposition themselves. As Hortense anticipates, migration to England would not only provide her with the needed social mobility, but it would also cause the "sun's heat on my face gradually change from roasting to caressing" (9) as she envisions connecting with different people and repositioning herself for the better.

Although there was a significant presence of ethnic minorities in Great Britain before World War II, the coming of these Jamaicans and many other members of former British colonies from 1948 onwards changed Britain in unprecedented ways. The socioeconomic and political changes that occurred as a result of the war created room for large-scale migration to England by former members of the British colonies. In the face of a dwindling economy occasioned by the war, the British government granted members of its former colonies free entrance into Britain to work to create a stronger economic base through the Nationality Act of 1948. As Andrian Favell notes, "Britain's peculiar relationship to the post-colonial Commonwealth ensured that, in this period, Britain maintained an opendoor relation to members of the Commonwealth who, as sovereign subjects, were effectively like British citizens with rights of entry and abode" (101). Although they were granted rights of entry and abode, they were denied full citizenship as they were treated as outsiders. The cold treatment, rejection of employment and housing, and other forms of discrimination from white British citizens made these immigrants realize that although they had viewed England as their "mother country," they were not wanted in England.

However, Black migrants have equally fought against their rejection and discrimination through riots and other forms of demonstration, such as the Notting Hill and Nottingham riots of 1958 that was spurred by racial tensions. These riots, in other words, gave rise to a new form of autonomous organizing within the black community as immigrants sought to protect themselves from further attacks. They provided them with the opportunity to begin to discuss their treatment in Britain and to redefine their social positions and racial identities. The result is their turning to their black cultural heritage and celebration of such.

Conversely, Blacks have also used their creative writing to question the various forms of segregation and discrimination they suffered in Britain. In so doing, they have been able to reconstruct not only their identities but also claim their British citizenship. Writing about the portrayal of West Indian immigrants by their white counterparts, Onyekachi Wambu states that "[U]p until 1948, the people of the region had been written about but had not sufficiently described their sense of self or their physical environment and landscape" (n.pg.). This is largely because Blacks were denied a voice of their own during the long period of slavery and colonization. However, post-war migration allowed them to begin to tell their stories and to demand the recognition of their humanity and voice even though they were marginalized at this historical moment as many of them came to Britain poor.

Conversely, although the black British community was able to create a little space for itself in the early postwar period, the presence of black British women was not so much felt as they were doubly displaced from British society and in literary canon as British publishers sought the writings of black men during this historic moment. However, the publication of black women's stories in the early 70s, such as Buchi Emecheta and Beryl Gilroy, helps to break their silence as they prove to the world that they have a story to share, just like their male counterparts. Their determination to build and nurture a new diasporic community attests to their resilience and resistance to their displacements and exclusion from British society. Excluded from the dominant history, black British women writers, as Gloria Anzaldua contends, continue to break down paradigms to create a new mythos—that is, "a change in the way we perceive reality, the way we see ourselves, and the ways we behave" (102). In so doing, they reconstruct from the dominant history their personal histories and narratives. Their stories, such as the novel Understudy, can, therefore, be seen as a response to Heidi Safia Mirza's call for women to "gather…the snippets of black women's stories as they emerge to challenge their negation and disrupt the neat telling of those stories" (7). Thus, their resilience, penchant for growth, quest for a new beginning, emplacement, formation of new identities and social relations and social repositioning are some useful factors needed in the construction of a rhizomatic womb-space as they continue to break their sociocultural barriers and push against the boundaries of exclusion to make room for their distinctive female stories and voices to emerge. Significantly is the fact that these black British women are not confined in their spaces of displacement but are opening these spaces for new stories and voices to emerge, just like the rhizome that produces new growth when injured.

Rhizomatic Womb-Space Theory[4]

Situating this study in postcolonial, gender, and migration studies, I explore the impact of migration on women and the contributions of Blacks, especially women, in the rebuilding and restructuring of British society in the post-war era using a rhizomatic womb-space theory as the major theoretical framework. The rhizomatic womb-space is a term I coined from Gilles Deleuze and Felix Guattari's concept of the rhizome, on the one hand, and from Ancient Greek theory of the wandering uterus/womb, on the other hand. The rhizomatic womb-space pushes for new social formations and relations that are informed by multiplicity, divergence, and connectivity. As Deleuze and Guattari explain in their introduction to *A Thousand Plateaus: Capitalism and Schizophrenia*, the rhizome gives room for multiplicity and interconnectivity and establishes a non-hierarchical relationship where different unrelated things are connected (6-7). The rhizome resists fixed points of emergence and rootedness. According to them, "when a rhizome is broken in one location, it emerges elsewhere with multiple openings and growths" (9). In this regard, a rhizome does not produce a single trait but leads to other connections, thereby creating multi-dimensional

---

[4] Part of this theory has been published in two other articles namely "The Migratory Female Subject and the Construction of Rhizomatic Womb-Space" and "Women Deconstructing History in Search of Their Own Voice and Identity in Zadie Smith's *White Teeth.*" (For more information on the rhizomatic womb space theory, refer to these articles as referenced on the Works Cited page).

assemblages that can come from one of its old lines or a completely new line. Thus, the rhizome defies any rigid classification as it seeks to disrupt even the root that produces it. In connecting the concept of the rhizome to the Ancient Greek theory of the "wandering womb" by such philosophers as Plato and Hippocrates, my goal is to show how women have not only resisted their subjugation but have also redefined themselves through migration and other cultural and social relations.

In Ancient Greek theory, the womb was seen as a living animal that was capable of moving about in the female body, and as a result, caused a lot of discomfiting problems to the female body and mind. In Plato's *Timaeus*, he describes the womb as a living animal desirous of childbearing, which is distressed when it is not fruitful; hence, it wanders in the female body:

> The so-called uteruses…in women—there being in them a living animal desirous of childbearing…whenever it is fruitless for a long time beyond its due season, being distressed it carries on with dificulty and by wandering in every direction throughout the body, by fencing off the passages of breath, and by not allowing (the body) to catch its breath, it throws it (the body) into the extremes of helplessness and provokes all other kinds of diseases. (Qtd in Faraone 3)

Not only does Plato describe the womb as a living animal desirous of childbearing, but he also portrays it in a negative light—as capable of causing pains in women when it is not sexually satisfied and also as one that can only be satisfied through its connection to the male. In essence, he frames the female body as dependent on men for its satisfaction, agency, and completeness. In Hippocrates' account of the wandering womb, he focuses on the different places the womb can attach itself and the various pains that come as a result of its wandering:

> If the uterus seems to sit under the diaphragm, the woman suddenly becomes speechless … and she experiences suffocation; she grinds her teeth and, when called, does not respond. When the womb strikes the liver or abdomen … the woman turns up the whites of her eyes and becomes chilled; some women are livid. She grinds her teeth and saliva flows out of her mouth. These women resemble those who suffer from Herakles' disease (i.e., epilepsy). If the womb lingers near the liver or abdomen, the woman dies of suffocation. (Qtd in Faraone 4).

Apart from Hippocrates' elaboration on the pains that the wandering womb causes women, he also considers the female body as physiologically cold and capable of producing humour or fluids, which must be purged. To stop the womb from wandering, therefore, different recommendations were made, ranging from getting married if the woman is single to keeping the uterus moist through constant sexual intercourse and stopping it from attaching itself to other moist parts of the body and, if married, to become pregnant. If the womb has wandered, it was recommended that baths, uterine infusions, and a series of physical manipulations and bindings of the abdomen be applied to force the womb back in place.

Contrary to the notion that the wandering womb affected women negatively by causing them hysteria[5], I have reconceptualized the womb as a productive space and used it to show the many ways women renegotiate their identities in different social positions they find themselves in society. I contend that the wandering womb, even in its representation in the Ancient Greek period, as the works of Plato and Hippocrates stated above show, is a subversive object that resists control and fixity and also creates its pathway as it wanders in search of moisture and satisfaction in other parts of the female body. In other words, the wandering womb has agency and defies any notion of fixity, origin, and rootedness as it moves about in search of its own identity and positionality. Significant is the fact that when the womb "wanders" from one place to another, it not only occupies a new position but also connects to other parts of the female body as well as adapts to new locations. In this regard, it becomes rhizomatic as it creates multiple identities for itself because it is not one part of the female body that is connected but multiple parts that meet at each point of contact.

Conversely, although the womb is no longer believed to wander, its original idea of constant mobility, rupture, displacement, reconnection, emplacement, and positionality informs my use of the womb space as a concept to explain the impact of migration on the migratory subject. Unlike its negative portrayal in Ancient Greek theory, the female body is not docile but is imbued with the power to question, renegotiate, and create something new. By re-appropriating the concept of the wandering womb, I explore how women can begin to redefine their identities by breaking barriers, charting their course, connecting with different people and taking new social positions in their new social milieu. Like the wandering womb, women who migrate reconstruct their identities through routes and various connections and contacts they make rather than through roots. In this regard, the rhizomatic womb-space pushes women to move outside the domestic sphere to which they have been confined to other areas of society to create new identities for themselves and to deconstruct every mechanism that confines them to a fixed position. In other words, it encourages women to defy fixed identities to opt for a more fluid identity formation.

---

[5] The term "hysteria" comes from the Greek word for uterus, "hysterika".

The rhizomatic womb-space, therefore, is a radical feminine space through which women not only critique those values that inhibit one's self-fulfilment but also offer new social relations, renegotiate their identities, and envision a new world built not on the "either/or" dichotomy that gender, class, race, and nationality evoke but on fluid identity and multiple connections. Thus, like the wandering womb that detaches itself from its original location to create a new space for itself, I contend that although women are displaced in various ways, their displacements offer them an opportunity to create new identities and spaces for themselves in their new social milieu. Their ability to place themselves in new places is a resilient act, which can be compared to the rhizome, which, when it is injured in one place, emerges with new growth in other places.

Although my conceptualization of a rhizomatic womb-space is informed by Deleuze and Guattari's concept of the rhizome and the Ancient Greek theory on the wandering womb, it also benefits from the concept of 'Third space' by Homi Bhabha and Edward Soja, especially in its construction as a radical and open space. Like Third space, it is informed by the constant search and desire to move outside the known or the established "truth" or "knowledge" to seek alternative reconstruction of the acceptable "truth" or "knowledge". As a concept, Third space pushes one to go beyond polarization or dualism to see how things can be done differently and in a new way. Rather than embrace a dualistic view, Third space advocates for the accommodation of the dualistic view and other ways of seeing or doing things. It also disrupts the notion of fixity as it advocates for openness to new ideas, meanings, events, and appearances. Thus, central to the understanding of Third space is the notion that there is no one singular way of doing things or seeing the world. Rather, it pushes one to understand and know that myriad new ways are opening up every day in the world, both politically, economically, socially, culturally, and geographically, that go beyond the fixed notions or polarization of things or ideas. Because the world tends to be structured to fit into a binary classification/categorization of an "either," "or" dichotomy, Third space breaks this dualistic tendency to create a different or third sense of the already established dualism. As Edward Soja notes, "Central to the understanding of Third space is the insight that there is not just one single definition of space and spatiality but rather a multitude of approaches and perspectives; all of them with new insights on the geographical imagination and the potential and limits to extend the scope of a critical geography" (50). Therefore, Third space is not to be understood as an alternative concept to the already existing approaches. Rather, it urges spatial thinkers to set aside the demands to make an "either/or" choice and contemplate instead the possibility of a "both/and also" logic. Similarly, the Third space is neither a physical space nor a unit of spatiality. Rather, it is a metaphor that is used to denote openness, a radical reinvention of ideas and conception of things. Metaphorically, it is a reaction against the dualism of ideas, personalities, conventions, approaches, perspectives, and objects.

One important concept that Soja uses to describe his conceptualization of Third space is "Thirding-as-Othering"—a concept he borrowed from Henri Lefebvre. According to Soja, the concept introduces a critical other than a choice that deconstructs all permanent constructions in its bid to reconstruct the already facts. As Soja notes, "Thirding introduces a critical 'other-than' choice that speaks and critiques through its otherness. In this regard, it does not derive simply from an additive combination of its binary antecedents but rather from a disordering, deconstruction, and tentative reconstitution of their presumed totalization producing an open alternative that is both similar and strikingly different" (61). The ultimate goal, therefore, is not merely to add to the already existing knowledge but to give room for a continuous search for new ways of doing and seeing things. The implication is that this "thirding" does not stop at the third term or notion but continues to expand in many other meaningful ways. Thus, the critical thirding can be described as a ground-breaking phenomenon that is geared towards deconstruction, recombination, reformation, reconstruction and reordering of a rigid dichotomy to open up other alternative ways and means to make practical sense of the contemporary world. It does so by expanding the already existing knowledge to provide alternative possibilities and meanings. For instance, in terms of social space, Third space provides alternative ways through which those who have been marginalized, and excluded from the dominant culture can resist their marginalized positions to renegotiate their identities. It, therefore, flourishes on a culture of difference and resistance.

The Third space of marginality, therefore, is a site of resistance rather than an acceptance of marginality. To live in the margin invariably implies living in a more diversified social space, as it allows one to interact with people from different social positions. It provides one with the opportunity to live, work, look, imagine, and understand the world from the outside in and from the inside out. Thus, the position of marginality, as Soja argues, is not one of powerlessness but one which the marginalized group reconstructs as they critique the dominant structure in their societies that fosters social division. It is rather a place of radical openness, critical thinking as well as resistance— where people resist all forms of subordination and oppression. As Bell Hooks contends, the margin is not a site one gives up or surrenders as one moves to the centre – but it is "rather... a site one stays in, clings to even because it nourishes one's capacity to resist. It offers to one the possibility of radical perspective from which to see and create, to imagine alternatives, new worlds" (207). The womb, though marginalized and subjected to different negative connotations in the Ancient Greek theory, is portrayed as a site of reformation geared towards creating new worlds and social relations.

However, unlike the Third space, the rhizomatic womb-space is migratory and feminine. It is concerned with how women's migration not only helps them reconstruct their identities but also opens new spaces as they move outside of their social categories and national boundaries. Apart from the fact that it is a social, mental, ideological, and creative space (some of these basic tenets it shares with Third space), it is also a biological space that involves the conception and nurturing of babies. In essence, the rhizomatic womb-space is concerned with how people are constructed in space and by space, as well as how new spaces emerge as people move from one place to another, question their identities, critique their social positions or positioning as well and differ from dominant ideological reasoning or conception. Also, it is concerned with the politics of dwelling and socialization, especially how people's location (be it a physical place or an ideological standpoint) shapes one's identity.

As a theoretical construct, the rhizomatic womb-space is defined as a site of radical openness that pushes for new social formations and relations that are informed by multiplicity, divergence, connectivity, and quest for change. It is a social, creative, intellectual, and ideological (feminine) space that is interested in questions of identity, gender, (un)belonging, and the critical interventions that women make in their immediate families and nations at large. It is also a biological space that explores the mother-child relationship and how women have been able to redefine the sociocultural and political landscapes through childbearing and rearing. In situating characters in a rhizomatic womb-space, therefore, what is important is not race, class, gender, or nationality but making connections, giving voice to the voiceless, redefining women's social positioning, and fostering new social relations geared towards creating a conducive environment for people as well as breaking not just one new ground but multiple ones as people begin to question and critique the binary oppositions that set them apart, create new spaces for minority voices to be heard and for minority stories to be retold.

Analysis

The rhizomatic womb-space that Hortense constructs through her journey and contacts with others is a sociocultural one. It is a space of dialogue, renegotiation, and reformation of the old values that place other cultures as inferior to European culture. As a black female migrant, Hortense is aware that she occupies the space of the margin, but she sees that as a space of resistance and power as she questions her inferior social position and places her culture and tradition alongside the European culture in her various dialogues with Queenie. It is from the marginal space that she begins to deconstruct the existing social relations and history to produce a new one. By constantly asking Gilbert if this is the way the English live, she not only refers to the demise of English culture and identity but also calls for its re-evaluation in line with other cultures competing with it. As Gilbert notes, Hortense's questioning of the English way of life becomes a refrain, a lamentation, and a constant reminder of her disappointment in the decay she sees in the once glorious British cultural heritage:

> Is this the way the English live? How many times has she asked me that question? I lose count...That question became a mournful lament, sighed on each and everything she saw. 'Is this the way the English live? 'Yes,' I tell her, 'this is the way the English live...there has been a war...She drifts to the window, looks quizzical upon the scene, rubs her gloved hand on the pane of glass, examine it before saying once more, 'This the way the English live' (18).

While Gilbert placates her by explaining the impact of war on everyone, all Hortense can see in their small room is decay, ruin, filthiness, darkness, displacement, disorderliness, and brokenness. However, despite Hortense's displacement on arriving in England and the deplorable conditions she finds their room and, by extension, British society, she is not ready to leave the society as it is but to get rid of the dirt and ruins to bring England to its glory, hence her first task of cleaning up the room beginning with the cracked sink, she then goes on to clean the stinking potty from under the bed. By ridding their room/society of its age-long socioeconomic, racial, and cultural dirt, Hortense makes room for a new world order devoid of the old social relations that have shaped Britain's relationships with colonized nations. The new world she fosters is informed by tolerance and accommodation of different cultural values, traditions, and individual perspectives. It is a new world order that is constructed from multiple histories, journeys, and cultures. Her constant questioning, therefore, becomes a metaphor for the need to "clean up" the dirt contained in the English culture and society manifested in racism, discrimination, segregation, and imperialism for the new world order to emerge.

The war, as Gilbert explains, destabilizes England in many ways, not only in terms of its economy but also in robbing it of its grandeur. The war brings England to "its knees" as it loses its overwhelming influence and power in the world. Bernard attests to the changes brought to bear on England's social milieu that subsequently led to its sudden disappearance when he declares, "I sat down to watch the spot where my country dissolved. It was there, etched on my eyes like an afterview of the sun" (334). The scene that Bernard describes shows the dissolution of the Empire and its loss of power and also speaks of Bernard's dislocation from his old culture. On returning to England after the war, Bernard sees a society ravaged by the war and steeped in irreparable losses. The damage is so great that he cannot recognize his country, "England had shrunk. It was smaller than the place I'd left" (350). But if the war has contributed to the ruin that Bernard sees, the presence of immigrants helped in its transformation as Blacks not only contributed towards building a stronger economy for the nation-state but also in constructing a multicultural British society. Unlike the pre-war moment when Blacks are considered as outsiders to British polity and history, Blacks see themselves as an integral part of the British nation during the post-war moment.

Hortense's journey to England depicts not only the desire of many immigrants to travel to England but also her desire to build a home in England, having been doubly displaced in Jamaica by her family background and her gender. Hortense explains that her father gives her away to his cousin to be brought up in the English way. Although she stands in between two cultures and identities, Hortense has always identified herself with the European culture and ideals. She expresses her sense of unbelonging in Jamaica and, as such, anticipates building her home in England. Her sense of belonging comes as a result of the colonial experience and education through which she has been taught to regard England as a mother country. As Levy explains in an interview, all the people in Jamaica are exposed to English cultures and ideals quite early in life. While in Jamaica, they are not only exposed to English culture and tradition but are meant to internalize these cultural values often at the expense of their own culture. As Levy notes in "This is my England," "Britain was the country that all Jamaican children learned about at school. They sang God Save The (sic) King and Rule Britannia. They believed Britain was a green and pleasant land—if not the centre of the world, then certainly the centre of a great and important Empire that spanned the globe, linking all sorts of countries into a family of nations" (n. pg). For Hortense and other Jamaicans, England is not only a centre of excellence or an epitome of civilization but a nation of power and wealth. In this regard, many of them envision England as their final destination and as the place they truly belong. As Hortense expresses when Gilbert decides to marry her and bring her to England, England is not only her home but her destiny: "I determined then to make this place somewhere to live...For England was my destiny" (187). Although they are in a nation that desperately needs their labour during the postwar period but wants nothing to do with their presence, Hortense and other black migrants are determined to build a home in England as well as be a part of its re-narration as it transitions to a multicultural society that is made possible through their presence, the birth of Queenie's biracial child and the multicultural society that he symbolizes, and their contribution to nation building, especially through their labour.

It is from her position as an insider that Hortense begins to remap and restructure the nation as she turns what Homi Bhabha refers to in "DissemiNation" as "the scraps, patches, and rags of daily life...into the signs of a coherent national culture" (209). She does this by resisting not only the various mechanisms used in the past to silence and displace Blacks but also by putting in place a new world order created out of diverse histories and voices. She begins by questioning Queenie's position and power as the landlady by blocking the entrance to the house with her trunk, thereby displacing Queenie from her usual position—a place of power and negotiation where she stands to welcome her visitors into her house/country or deny them access to it. In other words, by placing her trunk—a symbol of her belonging and demand for a cultural and political space—at the entrance of the door, Hortense does not require Queenie's permission to put in place her personal belongings and personal identity, as other immigrants do, but places them at the very position that Queenie stands to welcome or reject her visitors. Her trunk limits the free flow of movement and secures a diasporic and cultural space for her, both at Queenie's doorstep and in Gilbert's room. As Hortense tells everybody who cares to know what is in her trunk, she has brought everything she needs to build her home in England. As Duboin explains, the trunk indicates:

> The newcomer's will to take root in England and his/her unfulfilled quest for a stable location. In opposition to the house, the trunk is a symbol of movement and travel; yet it obstructs the passage and prevents the circulation of black and white, male and female dwellers competing for space and thereby for full recognition and a place in the 'Motherland' (18).

By putting on hold, temporarily, the free flow of human traffic and the possible discourses that take place at the doorstep, Hortense's trunk initiates a new dialogue geared towards repositioning immigrants and fostering social transformation. In so doing, she creates a Third space, a radical space, where cultural and personal identities are renegotiated.

Conversely, if one takes Queenie's house as an allegory of the nation, one sees the social transformation that takes place with the arrival of immigrants. As the novel reveals, Bernard's and Queenie's house is legendary because of its historical background. Reflecting on the importance of the room that Gilbert occupies in his house, Bernard notes that the room is not only important because of the many white births that it produces but also because of its vantage position as his mother sees the city from there. As Bernard explains, her mother not only uses this room for sewing, mending, and reading but also construes it as a feminine space of nurturing, as her husband rarely comes up there. In fact, Bernard's mother refers to it as "a woman's room" not only because of the many white births but also because of the added advantage it gives her to spy on her street and the rest of the world from that vantage position. In other words, it is a sociocultural and political space of transformation and social repositioning for Bernard's mother as it places her on top of her world (338).

Although the house is an enclosed space occupied only by white British citizens, Hortense and Gilbert's occupation of this room displaces Bernard from his homogenous white culture and the history that shapes it. In so doing, Hortense and Gilbert are placed above Bernard and Queenie, who live below them. Hortense notes that she has to climb many stairways to reach the room, and each step she takes moves her farther away from the ground and by implication, from Queenie and Bernard. The stairways, therefore, become a liminal space and a pathway to social elevation as Hortense and Gilbert rise above their social position as the "wretched of the earth." As Bhabha contends in *The Location of Culture*:

> The stairwell as liminal space, in-between the designations of identity, becomes the process of symbolic interaction, the connective tissue that constructs the difference between upper and lower, black and white. The hither and thither of the stairwell, the temporal movement and the passage that it allows, prevents identities at either end of it from settling into primordial polarities. This interstitial passage between fixed identifications opens up the possibility of a cultural hybridity that entertains difference without an assumed or imposed hierarchy (4).

Hortense's occupation of the room allows her to see the world from there. Like Queenie, whose father informs her after her encounter with the African man that the world is under her feet, Hortense's position at the house places the world under her feet as she is privileged to spy the world from there, just like Bernard's mother. By extension, she not only takes her place in British society but gazes back at its citizens.

The her-story[6] that Hortense reconstructs from this vantage point speaks of inclusion, especially of the minority voices and groups that she represents. More importantly, she subverts the racist ideology that Bernard and his likes embody. On many occasions, Bernard stands in strong opposition to the presence of Blacks in Britain. As he argues, after the war, "the war was fought

---

[6] Her-story is a term that denotes history written from a feminist perspective that portrays the experiences of women. It is an alteration of history as many feminist scholars believe that history was written from a masculine point of view and as such it becomes "his-story." Oxford English Dictionary defines it as "history emphasizing the role of women or told from a woman's point of view; (also) a piece of historical writing by or about women." Casey Miller and Kate Swift explain in their book, *Words and Women*, that "when women in the movement use herstory, their purpose is to emphasize that women's lives, deeds, and participation in human affairs have been neglected or undervalued in standard histories" (146).

so people might live amongst their kind. Everyone had a place. England for the English and the West Indies for these coloured people...I've nothing against them in their place. But their place isn't here" (388-9). But Hortense demonstrates that Blacks have come to stay and be a part of English society. Her-story as Stuart Hall contends, "breaks down boundaries, between outside and inside, between those who belong and those who do not, between those whose histories have been written and those whose histories they have depended on but whose histories cannot be spoken" (48). In other words, her rewriting of history becomes a rhizomatic womb-space through which she critiques the polar divisions that characterize British relationships with other nations.

Hortense's rewriting of history is a colonization in reverse. Significantly, the new narrative is told by a colonial subject and a black woman, two minority groups and identities that have been silenced in the British historical narrative. Her story marks the moment of transition, transformation, and change. Thus, while Levy notes that the war has brought many white people to their knees, she contends that it empowers immigrants as they are emboldened by their encounters with white people during the war to question their exclusion. Thus, the dissolution of the British Empire or what is metaphorically referred to in the novel as "the war bringing the Europeans to their knees" (341), helps to usher in a new social order, one that is built on respect and the recognition of the important roles different people play in rebuilding the nation. The war also makes it possible for immigrants to renegotiate their identities and build their diasporic homes as they move from their marginal position to the centre. Hortense references this sociocultural change when she notes how Queenie knees before her and Gilbert to beg them to take her biracial child. Not only does Queenie knee before them, but she also finds herself at the mercy of this black couple whom she needs to save herself from the shame of an extramarital affair with a black soldier that resulted in the birth of a biracial child. Like Bernard, her husband, the war also brings Queenie to her knees as she loses her domineering power during this moment of negotiation that determines not only her position in Britain but also that of her biracial child. This moment also captures the transformation that is taking place in Britain, especially in terms of social relations. It portrays a time in history when Britain is made aware that it can no longer continue to lay claim to its homogeneous culture but needs to come to equal terms with those other nations that have contributed to its growth and whose presence it can no longer ignore. On the other hand, it depicts the crumbling of the Empire as Queenie—the archetypal figure of Mother Country—has been brought to her knees by the war and its aftermath.

While Queenie is brought to her knees, Hortense is elevated to the status of a Mother Country when she accepts the responsibility of nurturing Queenie's biracial child as her own. In other words, while the changes taking place have brought white Britons to their knees in different ways, immigrants are rising above these challenges as they refuse to be brought down on their knees again regardless of their challenges. Gilbert attests to this when he tells Hortense that no wife of his will be on her knees for whatever reason: "I cannot see you on your knees so soon. I did not bring you to England to scrub a floor on your knees. No wife of mine will be on her knees in this country" (263). Thus, when Hortense and Gilbert leave Queenie's house, they have a house of their own and the new British national identity to nurture. Her final encounter with Queenie and her exit from Queenie's house marks her severance from the culture of exclusion and its homogeneity, as well as her silencing of Queenie—the old British Mother Country and all she represents to the black immigrant community. Explaining this final moment with Queenie, Hortense states she feels no sense of loss or longing for the house and all it embodies as she leaves its confines for a more inclusive space. Hortense ascendance to social mobility marks the decline of Queenie as well as her silencing and displacement from the evolving new British multicultural society. As Hortense explains, when she knocks on Queenie's door on her way to take possession of the new house placed in their care, Queenie hides behind her closed door: "At the door... I tapped gently three times. There was no reply. I tapped again, this time calling her name. Still no one came.... She was there—I knew" (438). Thus, unlike Hortense, who sees her marginal space as a site of power and resistance, Queenie's displacement leaves her trapped and powerless as the society transitions to a multicultural and multiethnic one.

It is also significant to note that it is from her position as the nurturer of a new nation that Hortense delivers Queenie, her baby. The child becomes the arc that connects Hortense to different places and things. The child connects her to Queenie and the British cultural heritage and becomes the bridge that links the domestic space to the public. Thus, by delivering and nurturing the baby, Hortense helps in the building of a new multiracial society that the child symbolizes. Conversely, she draws attention to the position of (Black) women in the reconstruction, reframing, and re-narration of British historical narrative and identity.[7] By performing these roles, Hortense silences and displaces Queenie and other male characters in the novel to occupy a prime place in the rewriting of history. By locking men out of the feminine space (the 'birthplace' where Queenie's child is delivered), she becomes the voice through which both the delivery of Queenie's biracial child and its underlying history are told. Thus, while Bernard and Gilbert are fighting over the custody of Gilbert's rented

---

[7] In *Imagined Communities*, Benedict Anderson argues that nationalism comes not so much from political ideologies but from cultural systems that preceded it. As such nations can be imagined and stories of origins of nationhood can be retold to create new boundaries.

room—a room associated with white births and British homogenous culture—Hortense and Queenie are creating an alternative space for a new birth of a nation and a people. The alternative birthplace is significant because it symbolizes rebirth, fluidity, and multiracial and multiethnic identities. In other words, this "'birthplace" becomes a liminal space[8] where identities are contested and renegotiated. It is at this 'birth-place' that Gilbert questions Bernard's racial identity, superiority, and homogenous culture to call for a need to work together to build and nurture a multiracial society that Queenie's child symbolizes.

The birth room, though a physical space, is also a radical and maternal womb space that alters the existing social relations as it produces new ones needed to build a multicultural British society. It is a place where new birth, ideas, identities, and growth are nurtured and brought to life. For instance, when Bernard tells Gilbert that he is unworthy to take care of Queenie's biracial child when Queenie pleads with him in the birth room to take him as his child, Hortense explains that Gilbert makes it known to Bernard that he, as a white Briton is not better than him, a black immigrant. In a moving speech, Gilbert goes on to inform Bernard of the contributions of Blacks to the rebuilding of a British nation during the war and afterwards warns him that failure to see him as an equal will lead to a continuous battle between them. He argues that having fought on the side of Britain during the war makes him a "legitimate" citizen, just like Bernard. For this reason, he refuses to buy into the master-slave relationship that shaped Britain's relationship with the colonies during the colonial era—a position that Bernard is pushing hard to maintain.

Although Bernard declines Gilbert's call to build a multicultural British society together, Queenie and Hortense understand the need to do so and work towards making it a reality. This is demonstrated in the child they deliver together. It must be stated that Queenie's encounter with the African man in the prologue changes her worldview, especially her perception and relationship with minority groups. Unlike Bernard, who refuses to change despite his encounter with the minority group during and after the war, Queenie's intracity movement connects her to different people and ideas that would later help her to develop an intimate relationship with Michael, a Jamaican soldier during the war and would also consequently lead to the conception of a biracial child. Thus, when Queenie and Hortense deliver the baby, they demonstrate not only the position of women in the restructuring and nurturing of a new British

---

[8] The term, "liminality" comes from Latin word "limen" which means threshold. In his 1960 book, *The Rites of Passage*, Arnold *Van Gennep*, defines it as a new beginning and a transitional step in rites of passage. For Van Gennep, to "cross the threshold is to unite oneself to a new world" (20).

society but, most importantly, the nurturing of a multiracial society in the womb space. They also bring to bear the role of women in nation-building, as the domestic space becomes a microcosm of the British nation. As Hortense informs Bernard when he insists that they let him into the house, "it's just a women's matter…No man is required at a birth but any fool could see why Mr. Bligh would be considered an intruder" (396). Hortense is bold to state categorically that the nurturing of future Britain lies in the hands of women, for the history that men have constructed is divisive and racial, as demonstrated in the argument between Bernard and Gilbert. Based on this understanding, she bars Bernard from entering into this maternal womb space of sociocultural (re)birth as she considers him an intruder to the new world order that women construct.

Conversely, although Queenie and Hortense work together to deliver the baby, Queenie leaves the narration and reconstruction of this maternal history in the hands of Hortense. As Hortense indicates, Queenie is only a vessel through which the much-awaited change comes. Hortense refers to the baby as "a new life for this world" and goes on to state "it was only I who could perform this… task" (399), of not only welcoming and nurturing the new nation that the boy symbolizes but also in severing the tie between Queenie and the baby as she cuts the umbilical cord. Thus, the rhizomatic womb-space that is opened through the birth of the child allows Hortense to rewrite the dominant history to incorporate the voices of women and other minority groups that have been silenced in the old historical narrative. Her discourse, as Bhabha explains in "DissemiNation," "contests genealogies of "origin" that lead to claims for cultural supremacy and historical priority" (225). Similarly, the alternative new space they create, therefore, is one in which the minority voice can begin to articulate and reshape British identity differently. It is also one that invokes a different history—one not informed by colonialism, imperialism, and unequal power relations but one constructed and informed by love and mutual respect. As Queenie informs the reader, the baby is conceived out of love and mutual understanding. However, Queenie is aware that her house cannot provide a home and the comfort the baby needs to take on the challenges ahead of him, hence her desire to give him away to Hortense and Gilbert.

Hortense's rhizomatic womb-space, therefore, becomes one that produces social bodies and social relations that are needed for the new British nation. By being a site for reformation and reconstruction of social relations rather than one that gives birth to biological children, Hortense transcends the traditional gender roles that limit women to child-bearing and rearing. In other words, by taking the responsibility of nurturing this new birth and the new nation that it symbolizes, Hortense bridges the gap between the domestic and the private spheres as she demonstrates that women can be actively engaged in the two spheres without compromising one or the other. This is one of the interventions of my rhizomatic womb-space theory to place women in different strata of society as they chart a new course for themselves. In this regard, Hortense's rhizomatic womb-space becomes a site for a new beginning for both Blacks and Whites as she welcomes all to this new space regardless of race, culture, nationality, ethnicity, gender, and sex. In many ways, she resists the racial stereotypes with which Blacks have been associated to create a space of dialogue, renegotiation, and reformation geared towards social change. Like a rhizome that is broken, Hortense's rhizomatic womb-space emerges not from a single trait of either Black or White ideology but from multiple openings and growths. Thus, the Hortense that one sees at the end of the narrative is one that has not only reclaimed her true identity but has also redefined herself as she embraces her Black cultural heritage and British identities, thereby making room for a fluid identity formation for her adopted child and a new British society that she nurtures in her rhizomatic womb-space. Her resilience and determination to build a new home in England, regardless of her many challenges, offers hope to many other minority groups who are faced with similar challenges as it encourages them not to give up in the fight for inclusion and racial justice.

Works Cited

Anderson, Benedict. *Imagined Communities: Reflections on the Origin and Spread of Nationalism.* Verso, 1983.

Anzaldua, Gloria. "Towards a New Consciousness." *Borderlands: The New Mestiza.* Aunt Lute Books, 1999, pp. 99-113.

Arnold, Van Gennep. *The Rites of Passage.* London: Routledge and Kegan Paul, 1960.

Baumeister, Andrea T. *Liberalism and the 'Politics of Difference.'* Edinburgh: Edinburgh University Press, 2000.

Bell, Hooks. *Feminist Theory: From Margin to Center.* South End Press, 2000.

Bhabha, Homi, *The Location of Culture.* Routledge, 1994.

---- "Dissemination: Time, Narrative and the Margins of the Modern Nation." *The Location of Culture.* Routledge, 2004. pp.199-244.

Bonnici, Thomas. "Diaspora in Two Caribbean Novels: Levy's *Small Island* and Philips' *A State of Independence.*" *Revista de Letras, Sao Paulo,* vol. 45, no. 2, 2005, pp 81-110. www.seer.fclar.unesp.br/letras/article/view/74.

Dawson, Ashley. *Mongrel Nation: Diasporic Culture and the Making of Postcolonial Britain.* Michigan: The University of Michigan Press, 2010.

Deleuze, Gilles and Felix Guattari. *A Thousand Plateaus: Capitalism and Schizophrenia.*Minnesota: *the* University of Minnesota Press, 1987.

Duboin, Corinne. "Contested Identities: Migrant Stories and Liminal Selves in Andrea Levy's *Small Island.*" *Obsidian: Literature in the African Diaspora,* vol. 12, no.1, 2011, pp. 14-33, www. hal.archives-ouvertes.fr/hal-00796225/document.

Ellis, Alicia. "Identity as Cultural Production in Andrea Levy's *Small Island.*" *Entertext: Special Issue on Andrea Levy,* vol. 9, 2012, pp. 69-83. www.brunel. ac.uk/__data/assets/pdf_file/0010/198064/6.

Evelyn, Kim. "Claiming a Space in the Thought-I-Knew-You-Place: Migrant Domesticity, Diaspora, and Home in Andrea Levy's *Small Island.*" *South Atlantic Review,* vol. 78, No. 3/4, 2013, pp.129-149. *JSTOR,* www.jstor.org/ stable/43739219.

Faraone, Christopher. "Magical and Medical Approaches to the Wandering Womb in the Ancient Greek World." *Classical Antiquity,* vol. 30, no. 1, 2011, pp. 1-32. *JSTOR.* www.jstor.org/stable/10.1525/ca.2011.30.1.1.

Favell, Andrian. *Philosophies of Integration: Immigration and the Idea of Citizenship in France and Britain.* Warwick: University of Warwick, 1998.

Fernandez, Irene Perez. "Representing Third Spaces, Fluid Identities and Contested Spaces in Contemporary British Literature." *Atlantis, Journal of the Spanish Association of Anglo-American Studies* vol. 31, no. 2, 2009, pp. 143-160. *MLA International Bibliography.* www.jstor.org/stable/41055369.

Hall, Stuart "Old and New Identities, Old and New Ethnicities." *Culture, Globalization and the World System,* edited by Anthony D. King, University of Minnesota, 2000, pp. 41-68.

Levy, Andrea. *Small Island.* London: Picador, 2004.

---Interview with Tracey Walters, "Andrea Levy." *Mosaic Literary Arts of the Diaspora,* 6 Nov.2011,https://mosaicmagazine.org/andrea-levy/.

--- "I started to realise what fiction could be. And I thought, wow! You can take on the world." Interview with Gary Younge, *The Guardian,* 29 January 2010. https://www.theguardian.com/books/2010/jan/30/andrea-levy-long-song-interview.

McLeod, John. "Postcolonial Fictions of Adoption." *Critical Survey* vol. 18, no. 2, 2006, pp. 45-55. *JSTOR,* www.jstor.org/stable/41556165.

Miller, Casey and Swift, Kate. *Words and Women.* New York: Harper Collins, 1991.

Mirza, Heidi Safia, editor. *Black British Feminism: A Reader.* Routledge, 1997.

Munoz-Valdivieso, Sofia. "Africa in Europe: Narrating Black British History in Contemporary Fiction." *Journal of European Studies,* vol. 40, no. 2, 2010, pp. 159-174.

Odoh, Ijeoma D. "The Migratory Female Subject and the Construction of Rhizomatic Womb Space." *The Comparative Media Journal,* Vol. 9, 2021.

---"Women Deconstructing History in Search of their Own Voice and Identity in Zadie Smith's *White Teeth.*" *Humanities Bulletin* Vol.3.No 2 Dec. 2020.

Perfect, Michael. "Fold the 'Paper and Pass it on': Historical Silences and the Contrapuntal in Andrea Levy's Fiction." *Journal of Postcolonial Writing,* vol. 46, no. 1, 2010, pp. 31-41.

Selvon, Sam. *The Lonely Londoners.* Longman Publishing Group, 1956.

Soja, Edward, "Thirdspace: Toward a New Consciousness of Space and Spatiality." *Communicating in the Third Space,* edited by Karin Ikas and Gerhard Wagner. Routledge, 2009, pp. 49-61.

Wambu, Onyekachi. "Black British Literature since Windrush." www.bbc.co. uk/history/british/modern/literature_01.shtml.

Chapter 7

Resilience as a Form of Contestation in the Poetry of John Clare

Anindita Chatterjee

Durgapur Government College, West Bengal, India

Abstract

The space can be perceived as a social product, 'determined by history, property and production'. (Henri Lefebvre). It implies an indication of stability and constancy intersected by the ensemble of movements deployed within it. John Clare, who was born in Helpston, has always been identified as a rural poet whose identity was deeply rooted in the topography of his native village. Ronald Blythe, commenting on his authenticity as a rural poet, observed that though the glory of the village landscape and native identity have always been highlighted in his works, it remains a fact that no other poet was more insulted or stigmatized in his lifetime for displaying it. In the critical reception of Clare, the context of social circumstances has often occluded his literary achievements. From the onset of Clare's literary career, readers have had to cope with the manner in which Clare's publishers sought to keep him rooted. He continues to share a liminal existence in the literary canon as a self-taught rural genius who was displaced from his home when the enclosure laws transformed the landscape of the place. There lies a seduction in the manner of viewing and constructing a narrative of his life that shuttles from home to homelessness, from a village in Helpston to the madhouse in Northampton, where he met with his end in 1864. Clare can be seen both as the poet of place and displacement, negotiating between a strong sense of self to a complete disintegration of identity. This paper would like to look into the journey of the wandering artist and explore the process of delocalising, which left his poetic self with no stable foundation, thereby resulting in an epistemological crisis. The primary focus of this paper would aim at establishing how Clare was a resilient voice who desperately hoped to outlive all stereotyped identification and make himself heard - an urge which made him proclaim, "I am—yet what I am none cares or knows" (Clare).

Keywords: John Clare, Space, displacement, homelessness, enclosure laws, resilience

***

Introduction

Any construction of identity, whether couched in terms of race, ethnicity, class or sexuality, necessarily involves a question of boundary and space. Henri Lefebvre is credited with defining the relational concept of space, which stemmed from social practices. Referring to perceived, imagined, and experienced notions of space, he claims that there is a fusion, intermingling and "co-existence of mental or ideal space along with the real or physical space" (14) and uses a theoretical framework to show how "each of these two kinds of space involves, underpins and pre-supposes the other" (14). Subjects are constructed through categorization, and these representations often become the precondition for all communication. Local attachments are integral to the understanding of Romantic poetry. According to David Simpson, English national identity became increasingly defined during the Romantic period "in terms of particular instances and local rather than cosmopolitan attachments in response to the association of the French Revolution" (139). In the case of John Clare, it is easy to construct a narrative of his life and creative works that traces a trajectory from home to homelessness, from a sense of integrated identity to complete disorientation and misgiving and an eventual fading into oblivion. The sense of place constitutes the root and essence of his poetry, which is evident in his capacity to find meaning and inspiration in the smallest details of his environment. The deracination of rural communities by the enclosure laws is also reflected in his work. Horkheimer and Adorno claimed that "Classification is a condition for cognition, and not cognition itself" (219) and emphasized how critique becomes necessary when socially dominant groups employ categories self-identically referring to something/someone in terms of themselves instead of referring to them on the basis of their own merit. They believed that all categories re-open to scrutiny and reformulation, for cognition in its real sense dispels simple labelling and general categorization. In the critical reception of Clare what we often tend to overlook is how Clare himself was always conscious of his marginalized status and estrangement right from the outset of his literary career. As Richard Cronin went on to observe, "Clare's localism was always troubled, always displaced, always on the verge of vanishing." (140)

Space and Poetic Identity

Identity is pragmatically linked to one's place of origin, language, ethnicity, gender and sexuality. It manifests itself in the creative consciousness. Per Aage, Brandt and John Hobbs, while charting the limits of poetic space, mentioned how the cognitive existence consists of not only one but three distinct imaginaries --a bio-imaginary, a socio-imaginary, and a phantasmatic imaginary.

> Space with its foregrounds (objects) and backgrounds (elements) is a grounding property of the imagination...We cognize and recognize ourselves as having sensitive bodies that breathe, sleep and wake, have a beating heart, and give us both pain and pleasure. The presence and the absence of other persons in this space of intimacy, is identified as the bio-imaginary. Presence and proximity are evaluated as euphoric whereas absence and distance are evaluated as dysphoric. The phantasmatic imaginary space is the one about which we recollect and revisit. The three spaces–that is the bio-imaginary, the socio-imaginary, and the phantasmatic imaginary – correspond closely to the experiential-semantic domains, oikos, polis, hieron as presented in Brandt (55).

In some poetic texts of John Clare, we find processes leading us through all of the three registers, the bio-imaginary, the socio-imaginary, and the phantasmatic imaginary, but at the same time, there exists an undercurrent wherein the poet defiantly seeks to rise above all the labels imposed upon him and assert his own distinctive individuality.

John Clare, the peasant poet

John Taylor's Introduction to Clare's first anthology, *Poems Descriptive of Rural Life and Scenery* (1820), was the first attempt to position him in the literary world. It read

> The following poems will probably attract some notice by their intrinsic merit; but they are also entitled to attention from the circumstances under which they were written. They are genuine productions of a young peasant poet, day labourer in the husbandry, who has no advantages of education beyond others of his class; and though Poets in this country have seldom been fortunate men, yet he is perhaps, the least favoured by circumstances, and the most destitute of friends, of any that ever existed (vii).

Taylor certainly aimed at chalking out the way for the poet's literary career, but in the intervening years, he has often been accused of not only "setting a patronizing tone for the reviewers of the volume" (Chirico 85) but also editing some of his linguistic experimentation and innovative material. In the ongoing controversy about the editing of Clare, many critics point out the editorial interventions to which the poet's textual embodiments were subjected. Nevertheless, it is true that being introduced to the world as the peasant poet, Clare has always been recognized for his commitment to his sense of place. In the words of Ronald Blythe:

> No other rural poet possesses his authenticity. None was more insulted in his lifetime for displaying it. And what a glory of place and native words has been shown to us. He is of all our poets the most intensely indigenous, a few fields and woods and wastes providing everything he needed for his exact response to their message (5).

His poetry has always been defined by a sense of perceptual particulars, of verisimilar imitations of nature. Being born into a near-illiterate impoverished peasant family in the village of Helpston, situated in Northamptonshire, Clare was deeply inspired by the landscape around him. Weiner claims that Clare often made use of local terms which were familiar in his Northamptonshire dialect and injected several polyphonous indigenous words into his verses, 'such as "pooty" (snail), "lady-cow" (ladybird), "crizzle" (to crisp) and "throstle" (song-thrush) and phrases like "waddled in the mud", "dimpling water pudge", and so on' (xii). Clare also went on to write about the figures in the margins 'like 'the humble bee', 'the bonny blackbird', 'the blythe milkmaid', 'the sooty crow', 'the pretty swallow' and the 'lonely shepherd boy', who wandered in the nameless thresholds and farmlands of Helpstone', (Weiner xii) thus charting out the contours of a utopic space, a community which constituted, defined, sustained and nurtured his identity. He described the familiar sights and sounds of the space around him from his keen and minute observation of nature and shared a sense of fellowship and empathetic understanding with the world and its living things. The use of the local dialect was integral to his poetic identity which enhanced the literary verisimilitude of the peasant poet. Considering Clare's commitment to specific locales, his critical reception stands upon this acute "sense of place" or *sui generis*. Justifiably, this has been the most prevalent perspective in the critical readings of Clare in the later years. Clare has always been presented as a self-taught rural genius because, like many other labouring-class poets whose geographical place and socio-economic positioning define their existence– his situatedness is the real mainstay behind his fame. The peasant poet Clare, who had been discovered in 1818 by Edward Drury, a Stamford bookseller, was introduced to the publisher John Taylor. Consequently, John Taylor presented Clare as a rustic genius in 1820 and basked in the glory, for he had discovered a natural genius, a self-taught poet. Taylor presented him as a poet who loves the fields, the flowers, the common air, the sun, and the skies. Most of Clare's poems were composed under the immediate impression of this feeling, in the fields or roadsides (Sychrava 94).

Taylor's "Introduction", which was an attempt to set up a robust and deliberate defence of Clare's poetic experimentation, still serves as a predominant signifier by which the poet John Clare is read to date. Through it, the peasant -poet John Clare was included in the same league as Robert Bloomfield, Stephen Duck and Robert Burns, who were all branded as pastoral rural bards. Stephen Duck wrote a poem in 1730 called "The Thresher's Labour", which initiated a new tradition of peasant-poet in the eighteenth century. Clare's publishers, too, were trying to capitalize on this popular trend of peasant poetry, which had been popularized by a generation of poets like Burns and Bloomfield, who had emerged in the literary scene dreaming of social inclusivity composing verses with the intention of establishing the fact that one can be a poor farmer or labourer as well as a creative poet at the same time.

Clare, the Rural Bard

Clare's critical reception has always been based on the label which was assigned to him from the outset of his literary career. Introduced to the world as an agricultural labourer and peasant-poet, Clare is identified, to this day, as an ecopoet whose identity remains deeply embedded in the natural world in which he lived. He inhabits a hyphenated marginalized space, and as a self-taught rural bard, he wrote descriptive pastoral poems in his early years. Since his first publication, readers have been instigated to read and accept him as a "peasant poet" culturally bound to his particular class and landscape. Clare's poem "The Peasant Poet" is largely autobiographical in spirit. He was aware of his own lineage and knew his fortune was not promising enough to adopt a professional poetic career. Being a thresher's son, he was destined to become a ploughman, a thresher, a gardener, or a lime burner like his ancestors, and so his identity was always fraught with the crisis of being confined to the liminal space of being a peasant poet and a deep-rooted yearning to transcend it. In his lyric "The Progress of Rhyme", Clare wrote, "My harp though simple was my own/ when I was in the fields alone" (lines 1-2) and described how the "Fields were the essence" (line 3) of his songs. They were his "real teachers" who had inspired his verses. As Merryn and Raymond Williams observe,

> it was taken for granted that a peasant poet was uneducated in a deliberate and specializing sense. Being uneducated implied a lack of the knowledge of formal grammar, yet at the same time it ensured a power to break through established conventions, a freshness and a

spontaneity of observation and feeling, the qualities that had supposedly been lost in the movement to a more artificial way of life and culture (5).

The sonnets written during the middle period of his literary career show how structures and identity correspond to numerous aspects of the natural world, which is bound by human experience. Experience is by turns unified and disordered, bounded and infinite, and so these poems mirror some of the dominant concerns that defined Clare's poems, which he wrote at Helpston and Northborough. These poems reflect upon his anxieties regarding his sense of place and time. They negotiate between his private and public worlds and show how he was affected by the movement of people, transience, and memories, and hence tried to hold on to the images of birds and animals that pervaded the landscape. Many of his poems bring out a desperate concern to hold on to the idea of an idyllic paradise, which he believed would soon be lost and gone.

Clare's prose has been generally neglected by critics, which is certainly a serious omission as there are passages replete with rich, complex, and psychologically sensitive observations which are no less significant than any of Wordsworth's reminiscences of spots of time. Clare's writings bring out a restructuring of the memories of liminal moments when the self is bewildered and often finds itself out of place, as well as driven by an impulse that seeks to explore the unseen and unknown trajectories. In an autobiographical passage written by Clare collectively published in *John Clare by Himself* (2002), he mentions his frequent escapades into the open fields of nature. He goes on to write-

> I loved this solitary disposition from a boy and felt a curiosity to wander about the spots where I had never been before…. when the white moth had begun to flutter beneath the bushes the black snail was out upon the grass and the frog was leaping across the rabbit tracks on his evening journeys and the little mice was nimbling about and twittering their little earpiercing song with the hedge cricket whispering the hour of waking spirits was at hand which made me hasten to seek home I knew not which way to turn but chance put me in the right track and when I got into my own fields (40).

The passage begins as "I loved" and then wanders off into the details of his sojourn when he ventures out alone, and describes how his parents were anxious about him in his absence. There was a sense of excitement, wonder, and anxiety in his works and an intense attachment to the landscape of the place which were the hallmark of the romantic artist. In a temper that almost reminds us of the wandering lonely child in Book 1 of Wordsworth's *Prelude*, Clare goes on to refer to his vivid observations of the landscape around him. He sought solitary pleasure exploring the local and familiar, and the passage brings out the delight of the child at the prospect of discovery and exploration. The fact that Clare's core identity revolved around his local space features prominently in the poetry written in his later years wherein he writes about his lost childhood with greater specifics. It has been suggested that Clare's psychological breakdown was brought about by cumulative forces, and one of the primary reasons among them was the trauma of truncation from his roots as well as the claustrophobic strictures of the English class system.

The Impact of Enclosure Laws

With the advent of the new enclosure laws John Clare's life was affected by the change of circumstances. The lyrical poems written by him during the post-enclosure period bring out a vivid portrait of the effects of displacement and dislocation upon the rural community. There is a constant negotiation between the being and becoming, a craving for the pre-lapsarian world of innocence marked by a severe sense of dispossession and loss. The poems exhibit an injury, a trauma and an aching for home. In his account of the *Journey out of Essex,* which records the poet's experience of escape from Allen's asylum in 1841 in a desperate attempt to return home, Clare wrote, "So here I am homeless at home and half gratified to feel that I can be happy anywhere." (Haughton 1). These words point to his lifelong struggle of trying to find a place for himself. The dislocation and internal migration had brought about a biochemical imbalance in Clare's mind, which also affected his sense of identity as a person and an artist. Many critics believe that a major cause of his mental breakdown was triggered by the establishment and enactment of the Enclosure Laws, which called for a dislocation of space. Since Clare's poetry was strongly defined by his roots, the loss of a familiar landscape psychologically disoriented him. Dislocation or displacement from the roots of origin, whether under compulsion or as a deliberate act of intention, is no less than calamity. It fosters an eerie and uncomfortable sense of un-housedness. This sentiment is common among people who might have either willingly or forcefully moved from their homes and places of belonging to new locations. This initial sense of unbelonging is reflected in the nostalgic reminiscences and poetic lamentations as one strives to cope with the new space. The poems written by Clare during this period are predominantly concerned with the issues of the fractured self and are replete with nostalgia and identity-crisis. Apart from a sense of personal loss, they also bring out "the indignation at the curtailment of the ancient rights within his community." (Bate 347) Although there are debates about whether Clare's breakdown was entirely affected by the social changes or not, it remains a fact that his creative instincts were definitely influenced to a large extent by the eradication of his childhood oasis, for it is an undeniable fact that an earnest quest for self-identity constitutes the central praxis for an individual's social existence.

Critical reception of Clare

According to John Barrell, while most writers of landscape poetry in the late eighteenth or early nineteenth century saw the world as a view from afar, "John Clare always saw his home from the level of the ground". (Barrell 172). Clare was guided by principles similar to that of the rustic bard James Hogg, who believed that simplicity was the most important aspect of poetic creativity.

> Take the simplicity of Moses, the splendour of Job, David, and Isaiah. Take Homer, and if you like, Hesiod, Pindar, and Ossian, and by all means William Shakespeare. In short, borrow the fire and vigour of an early period of society, when a nation is verging from barbarism into civilisation; and then you will imbibe the force of genius from its original source (103).

While it cannot be doubted that simplicity was a hallmark of Clare's identity, a quality that he shared with the prophet and the visionary, it was also a fact that this was not necessarily limited to his rural background. Yet, at the same time, it still remains a fact to date that it is essentially the identity of being a self-taught rural peasant poet is how he features in the literary canon. His critics and editors had tried to create an image of the man, and it has deeply influenced the way his poetry has been perceived and read to date. Clare tried to surpass this classification but failed. Living in Victorian England, negotiating with class consciousness and marketing strategies, he did not have the power to transcend them all. Hence, Clare's position in the critical canon has always been fraught with uncertainties and arguments. Incidentally, Clare wrote a lyric in his early years entitled "The Fate of Genius". Little did he know how the lines would become true and prophetic in his own life.

> Here sleeps the hopes of one whose glowing birth
> Was found too warm for this unyielding earth.
> (lines 127-128)

Harold Bloom, in his *The Visionary Company*, identified Clare as a "Wordsworthian Shadow" whose destiny resembled the fate of minor poets of all ages who are forced to live and write under the shadows of their influential predecessors. Kelvin Everest, in his *English Romantic Poetry*, observes how "Clare still remains an underrated and relatively neglected figure." (14) He remained something of "a backwater poet" and could never become a part of "mainstream English Poetry." (Haughton 11). Hugh Haughton mentioned how Edmund Blunden, writing on John Clare a century after his death in 1964, felt that the Northamptonshire Peasant poet "is too little known and perhaps is one of the few English writers most difficult to estimate." (11) Clare's poetry bears evidence of his emotional and mental turmoil and struggle for existence. Clare's experience, according to Tom Paulin, is similar to the modern notion of apartheid. Clare was segregated from the literary world, which made him feel like an outcast or perhaps a black slave chained in plantation. Clare believed that slavery

> was "disgraceful to a country professing religion", and it would seem that at some level he felt himself to be a slave who had mistaken the brief kiss of fame for a lasting manumission (50).

In a humorous poem entitled "Clare's Jig", Ian Duhig (1999) goes on to describe John Clare's independent and resilient spirit that sought to defy the norms and impositions of editors and critics in order to assert its own identity.

> I'd collected a good jig called "The Self"
> but lilting it last night for Dr. Bottle
> he chided me, opined it should be Sylph,
> which is Greek, like much he says, meaning beetle.
> He chokes the same and gibbets butterflies,
> now all your rich men's fashionable rage.
> My fellow inmates praise him to the skies,
> and like a hawk he scans my every page,
> the dumb Morris of these poor whopstraw words.
> When pressed, a melancholy John son said
> "Why Sir, we are a nest of singing birds!"
> Well, I hear boughs breaking inside my head
> So, listen till the music has to stop
> For like a tree, I'm dying from the top.
> (lines 1-14)

It is for this reason that many Clare critics like Mina Gorji argue that there has always been a problem concerning the critical reception of the poet. The "social placing" (122) Clare has been over-emphasized to such an extent that it becomes difficult for readers to see him beyond the identity imposed upon him. "Too much attention has been focused on his social circumstances in ways that often risk occluding his literary achievements" (Gorji 122). Clare, as Tom Paulin points out, was the

> displaced, marginalized poet whose reputation is gradually being rehabilitated—as Mandelstam's is in Soviet Union. It may be many years, though, before his name is given the kind of official recognition which is accorded to Wordsworth and Keats...But it could be that Clare—shy, feral, intensely gifted—will never be redeemed from all the neglect and mutilation he has suffered (Paulin 48).

The publication of Frederick Martin's biography established him as a man who was victimized by society and the literary world, and in a way, his life echoes the fate of John Keats and Bloomfield. Martin tries to evoke sympathy for the rural bard who became a lost voice with time and consequently, John Clare went on to become a romantic icon with time. As Martin observes,

> The Northamptonshire Peasant was duly petted, flattered, lionized and caressed, and of course as duly forgotten when his nine days were passed. It was the old tale, all over (10).

Martin's biography recounts how, in the mundane spaces at the edges of the field, Clare found not only rest and succour but also poetic inspiration and identity and how the disruption and re-orientation of the landscape with the enclosure laws immensely affected his life, mental stability and creativity.

> Unlike the rising number of migrant wageworkers in the early 1800s, his family was attached to the village of Helpston and therefore had certain rights to live and to work. The process of enclosure did not only take away his right to a piece of "land;" it also took away his right to a particular way of life: a way of life that moved between field and waste, the aesthetic and the practical, and private and common land (Holmes 2).

Clare was admitted to the County Lunatic Asylum in Northampton in 1841 after he was diagnosed with manic depression and mental instability. According to critics like Evan Blackmore, Clare's mental condition was similar to that of a patient with "bipolar disorder" (227), which exerted various complex influences on his poetry. It may, at times, have modified his literary productivity or disrupted the coherence of his writing. "The disorder and its social consequences almost certainly sharpened and personalized his view of human suffering'. (Blackmore 227).

Clare's tragedy was that he was a misfit everywhere. Though he was not an overreacher with poetic ambitions, nevertheless, he was caught in an irresolute conflict between the two identities imposed upon him, and he was resolute to protest and rise and defy the stigma of the labels which were imposed on him. There lies a seduction in the manner of viewing and constructing a narrative of his life that shuttles from home to homelessness, from a village in the remote corner of Helpston to the madhouse in Northampton, where he met with his end in 1864 after twenty-seven years of confinement. Clare can be seen both as the poet of place and displacement, negotiating between a strong sense of self to a complete disintegration of identity.

The neglect and pain that had wracked his mind finally found expression in perhaps one of his most sublime poems, which proclaims his fierce sense of resilience and resolve is "I Am":

I am —yet what I am, none cares or knows;
My friends forsake me like a memory lost:
I am the self-consumer of my woes:
They rise and vanish in oblivion's host,
Like shadows in love's frenzied, stifled throes: —
And yet I am, and live— like vapors tossed

Into the nothingness of scorn and noise, —
Into the living sea of waking dreams,
Where there is neither sense of life or joys,
But the vast shipwreck of my life's esteems;
Even the dearest, that I love the best
Are strange–nay, rather stranger than the rest.

I long for scenes, where man hath never trod
A place where woman never smiled or wept
There to abide with my Creator, God,
And sleep as I in childhood, sweetly slept,
Untroubling, and untroubled where I lie,
The grass below—above the vaulted sky.
(1-18)

The more the poet became confused and baffled in frustration and agony, with his economic distress, lack of support from publishers, ill health, and mental agony, the more passionately he proclaimed, "I Am" . The poem not only describes a moment of loss of self, it also proclaims a regeneration of spirit and a Shelleyian echo of "If winter comes can Spring be behind?"[1] It is a moment that at once bespeaks a loss as well as a resilient bouncing back to find a revival of the poetic self. The poem delineates the existential anxiety of the poet. It aches about a permanent loss and has enshrined Clare's place in the Romantic lore, providing the world with an archetypal image of the artist as a terminally tortured and alienated soul pitted against a hostile world and benumbing reality. The poem presents Clare as an oracle of modern identity. The confessional approach brings out his true pain, and we can trace the plight of the man behind the walls of the asylum. The poem is noted for its stark, blatant note of anguish, dejection and distress. It is also an assertion of identity, an address to the world that the poet had left behind, a world of his old friends, family and love, colleagues, critics and admirers. Clare seems resolute and determined to affirm his continued existence to them. It seems that he intends

---

[1] The lines have been taken from Shelley's "Ode to the West Wind" (1819). The phrase far behind is used to denote that spring, symbolising hope, regeneration and renewal is never far even in the depths of bleak winter.

to proclaim to the world that despite the rude blows that he had suffered in life, despite his diminished condition, he had still managed to survive. As David Barber notes, "In its delicately modulated syntactical conjunctions, nuanced precision of its semantic qualifications, the hammer blows of the title phrase repeated four times in the initial six lines, the agile alternating rhyme scheme that constrains its two sinuous periodic sentences, both coming to rest in resonantly toiling couplets," [2]the power of this poem can be experienced. The last stanza of the poem almost becomes a fervent prayer, an impassioned plea for restitution of lost paradise. It is an avid yearning for bygone blissful memories, a hope for redemption. It is, in fact, a breathless vision of transcendence.

Incarcerated within the walls of the asylum, negotiating with the label of insanity, John Clare attempted to rewrite Byron's *Childe Harold* and *Don Juan*. He began impersonating the adventures of a Byronic hero. It is difficult to accept that the poems were written during an unstable mental condition. Clare wrote about forbidden pleasures vicariously by identifying himself with the imagined persona. *Don Juan* was Clare's masterpiece, and, according to many, it was a work of boundless genius.

> there is a strong element of satiric force in the poem. Byron can, and does, call attention to the gulf between what people say, they believe, and their actual behaviour; hypocrisy becomes the main target of his satire. Accordingly, the centre of positive value in *Don Juan*, as in the plays, is freedom. His bitterest attack, found in the cantos on the siege of Ismail, is on the false glory of war. (Mc Connell 417)

Clare's *Don Juan*, written in imitation of Byron, expresses the poet's erotic fancies and discontent with the hypocrisies and the repressive attitudes of the age, which denied and suppressed sexuality. Dormant desire, frustrated passion, the trauma of failure and the agony of loneliness gave birth to Clare's bitterness. According to Jason N. Goldsmith (2006), "Clare's use of obscene and vulgar sexual puns corresponds to the Regency taste in punning" (810), which he acquired from Rippingale and "it forms a part of a concerted, if not entirely coherent, response to a culture increasingly organized by the spectacle of celebrity." (810) Negotiating the complex relationships between poverty, literary fame and financial security, Clare's *Don Juan* was aimed as a criticism against the shallow and insincere politeness of English society and its vain manners. The poem denounces the literary canon, poetic identity, and critical

---

[2] Barber, David. 1999. "On John Clare's "I Am", posted on December, 8th, in http://www.theatlantic.com/unbound/poetry/soundings/clare.htm. The verse "I Am" has enshrined Clare's case history in Romantic tradition, providing us with an archetypal image of the artist as a terminally tortured soul. The poem brings out the existential angst and social alienation of Clare.

practice since Clare felt that critical acclamation was severely biased and opinionated, which made it difficult for a lesser-known creative individual to find a place for himself. Clare's reworking of Byron's *Don Juan* bears within it the signs of his own troubled relations with the reviewers and publishers, for Clare wanted to resist the stigma of the label of being a Northamptonshire Peasant poet. Clare had to bear and deal with the oxymoronic reputation of being a "peasant poet", which, according to him, was an explicitly non-canonical category.

Conclusion

Simon Kövesi (2017), in *Masculinity, Misogyny and the Marketplace: John Clare's Don Juan*, mentions the two inscriptions engraved on the poet's grave. On one face of the gravestone in the church yard of St. Botolph in Helpston, where the poet is buried, these words are inscribed, "poet is born not made" (77). These words owe their origin to *Don Juan*. On the other side appear a few more words, "A Northamptonshire Peasant Poet", an identity which derives its origin from his life. It was imposed upon him by his publisher, John Taylor, who sought to establish Clare's fame as a natural genius, a Wordsworthian Child of Nature. Clare still continues to exist in the confusing limbo between these two imposed identities. He sought to transcend his humble origin, for his literary merit was far above the class of a common rustic farmer; he was introduced to the world as a self-taught genius. It is true that his identity was deeply rooted in his consciousness of the space around him but he was more gifted than what he has been given credit for. Yet, ironically enough, to date, Clare continues to exist in a no man's land. He is neither Romantic nor Victorian, neither a simple rural versifier nor an established major poet in the canon. He continues to pose problems before the literary world and his asylum verses still baffle critics as well as readers. Despite the binaries that define him and the debates that surround him, it cannot be denied that Clare struggled to remain true to his self-till the end of his life. His language reveals his own devastation. His poems survive as remains, offering intimation of his loss, anguish and annihilation.

Works Cited

Barrell, John. *The Idea of Landscape and the Sense of Place* 1730–1840. Cambridge UP. 1972

Bate, Jonathan. *John Clare: A Biography*. Picador. 2003.

Blackmore, Evan. "John Clare's Psychiatric Disorder and Its Influence on His Poetry", *Victorian Poetry*, Vol. 24, No. 3 (Autumn), pp. 209-228. Accessed from https://www.jstor.org/stable/40001184. 1986.

Blythe, Ronald. "A Message from the President", *John Clare Society Journal*, 1, 5, p 5. 1982.

Brandt, Per Aage. "The Architecture of Semantic Domains". *Spaces, Domains, and Meaning. Essays in Cognitive Semiotics*. Bern: *European Semiotics*, 4, Peter Lang Verlag. 2004.

Brandt and John Hobbs, "Elements in Poetic Space". *Cognitive Semiotics* 2 (Supplement) DOI:10.1515/cogsem.2008.2. Spring2008.129. 2008

Chirico, Paul. "Authority and Community: John Clare and John Taylor". *Authorship, Commerce and Public*. Palgrave. 2002.

Clare, John. *Poems Descriptive of Rural Life and Scenery* with an Introduction by John Taylor. London: Taylor and Hessey. 1820.

---- *Selected Poetry and Prose* edited by Merryn and Raymond Williams. London: Routledge. 1986.

---- John *Clare By Himself*. Edited by Eric Robinson and David Powell London and New York: Routledge. 2002.

Cronin, Richard. "In Place and Out of Place: Clare in *The Midsummer Cushion*". *John Clare: New Approaches*. Eds. John Goodridge and Simon Kövesi. John Clare Society. pp 133-48. 2000.

Duhig, Ian. "Clare's Jig". *John Clare Society Journal*, Number 18, July, 1999 pp 49-51. 1999.

Everest, Kelvin. *English Romantic Poetry: An Introduction to the Historical Context and the Literary Scene*. Liverpool UP 1990.

Goldsmith, Jason N. "The Promiscuity of Print: John Clare's "Don Juan" and the Culture of Romantic Celebrity", *Studies in English Literature 1500-1900*, Number 4, Volume 46, Autumn 2006 pp 803-832. 2006.

Gorji, Mina. *John Clare and the Place of Poetry*. Liverpool UP. 2008.

Haughton, Hugh, Adam Philips and George Summerfield. Eds. *John Clare in Context*. Cambridge UP. 1994.

Hogg, James, Gillian Hughes and Douglas S. Mack. Eds. *A Series of Lay Sermons on Good Principles and Good Breeding*. Edinburgh University Press. 1997.

Hughes, Gilliam. "I think I shall soon be qualified to be my own editor: Peasant poets and the Control of Literary Production", *John Clare Society Journal*, Number 22, July, pp 6-7. 2003.

Holmes, Eliza. "John Clare: Scavenger Poet" *Interdisciplinary Studies in Literature and Environment*, October, pp. 1–23. 2020.

Horkheimer, Max and Theodor Adorno. *Dialectic of Enlightenment*. Continuum. 1991.

Kövesi, Simon. *John Clare: Nature, Criticism and History*. Palgrave. 2017.

Lefebvre, Henri. *The Production of Space*. Blackwell. 1991.

Martin, Frederick. *The Life of John Clare*. Macmillan. 1865.

Mc Connell, Frank D. Eds. *A Norton Critical edition of Byron's Poetry*. Norton. 1978.

Paulin, Tom. *Minotaur: Poetry and the Nation State*. Faber and Faber. 1992.

Simpson, David. *The Academic Postmodern and the Rule of Literature: A Report on Half-Knowledge*. University of Chicago Press. 1995.

Sychrava, Juliet. *From Schiller to Derrida Idealism in Aesthetics*. Cambridge UP. 1989.

Weiner, Stephanie Kuduk. *Clare's Lyric: John Clare and Three Modern Poets*. Oxford UP. 2014.

Williams, Merryn and Raymond. Eds. *John Clare: Selected Poetry and Prose*. Methuen. 1986.

Chapter 8

Mise en Abîme: A Strategy that Highlights a Wandering, Fluid Subjectivity in Abdallah Laroui's novel *'Awrāq: Sīrat Idrīs al-dhihniyyah*

Anouar El Younssi

Oxford College of Emory University

Abstract

This essay probes the question of subjectivity-in-the-(re) making in Moroccan writer Abdallah Laroui's 1989's "novel" *'Awrāq: sīrat Idrīs al-dhihniyyah* (Papers: Idrīs's Intellectual Biography). *'Awrāq* is a two-layered text, presenting the reader with, first, a stack of papers of various sorts belonging to the diseased protagonist Idrīs, and second, the commentaries on this archive by two key characters. The book constantly oscillates between these two layers, attempting in the process to shake the dominant realist form and its underlying European point of reference. *'Awrāq*'s search for its best form parallels Idrīs's quest to restore his identity and subjectivity in the context of France's colonial project and legacy. The book's constant oscillation between narration and commentary is in line with its endeavour towards formal deformation, a penchant that foregrounds *'Awrāq*'s cultural and socio-political anxieties. The subversion of narrative forms turns out to be pivotal for laying the ground for the emergence or flourishing of a new type of "subject"—what Laroui calls *al-mawḍū'* in Arabic—and a renewed/refashioned subjectivity. Importantly, just as Idrīs wrestles with his identity vis-à-vis his new place of residence (Paris) and the European philosophical tradition he studies, *'Awrāq* wrestles with its ideal form. The term "intellectual biography" in the book's title alerts the reader to the formal and political threads running through the book. This seemingly unorthodox nomenclature ("intellectual biography") is in line with the aspiration to forge a new subject and a renewed subjectivity. In this respect, the politics of form intersects with the book's ideological bent: its endeavours to mould new literary configurations to grapple with questions of culture, politics, and identity in Morocco's postcolonial era. The bearing of form on thought is here brought into sharp focus. For Laroui, how we write literature is vital and indispensable in constructing new horizons to treat critically the challenges facing not only the individual but also the collective, in this case, the Moroccan nation(state) or Arab civilization more broadly.

Keywords: Subject, Subjectivity, Form, Deformation, Aesthetics, Politics, Morocco

***

Introduction

Abdallah Laroui's novel *'Awrāq: sīrat Idrīs al-dhihniyyah*[1] (Papers: Idrīs's Intellectual Biography) is a seminal work in contemporary Moroccan literature. Its publication in 1989 consolidated the experimental turn in Moroccan literary writing in the postcolonial era, i.e., post-1956, the year Morocco attained political independence from France and Spain. Viewed through the lens of mainstream novelistic tradition in Morocco, Laroui's *'Awrāq* stood out in large part thanks to its "profound experimentation" and its endeavours to strike "a unique and authentic artistic reconciliation between form and content" (Al-ʿUmrānī qtd. in El Younssi 190). It was deemed an important addition to a burgeoning literary strand that littérateurs in Morocco named *al-tajrīb* (experimentation), "a new phase in Arabophone Moroccan literary history" that arguably lays "the ground for a different vision of literature in postcolonial Morocco" (El Younssi 190). This experimental turn seeks "to overstep the 'traditional' model of Moroccan novelist ʿAbdulkarīm Ghallāb (1919–2017), which was inspired by the formidable oeuvre of Egyptian Nobel Laureate Najīb Maḥfūẓ (1911–2006)" (190). In brief, within this experimental turn, "narrative linearity and verisimilitude" are abandoned and "[f]igural depictions of plausible worldly coordinates are less important"; instead, the new experimental texts, such as Laroui's *'Awrāq*, are "marked by the formal, structural, and linguistic invocation of new subject positions and their immediate political exigency" (190—191). These new subject positions or positionings are indicative of Moroccan experimental literature's endeavours to create new discursive spheres for the

---

[1] This book was first published in 1989 and went through a number of editions. It was translated into French as *Les carnets d'Idris* in 2007. Thus far, it has not been translated into English. Throughout this essay, I will refer to the book as *'Awrāq* and will refer to the author by his Latinized name Abdallah Laroui. I should note that all translations from the Arabic are mine.

treatment of the social and the political. The exploration of the vicissitudes of subjectivity/subjectivities within the literary text takes centre stage.

This chapter probes the question of subjectivity-in-the-(re)making in Laroui's novel *'Awrāq*, focusing on the workings of the narrative device of *mise en abîme* as it relates to the resilience (or lack thereof) and ever-evolving subjectivity of the novel's deceased protagonist Idrīs. *'Awrāq* is a two-layered text that includes a collection of papers of various sorts, drafted by the late Idrīs as well as commentaries on this Idrīsian archive by two additional key characters, the Narrator and Shu'ayb. Laroui's *'Awrāq* shifts between these two modes of narration—as it attempts to unsettle or disrupt the realist writing model and its underlying European framework. Thus, the novel's quest for its ideal form goes hand in hand with Idrīs's interrogation of his identity and subjectivity in the context of France's colonial enterprise and legacy. While a Moroccan national and deeply invested in his nation's aspiration to be liberated from French (and Spanish) colonial rule, Idrīs did move to France/Paris to pursue his university studies before Morocco had not yet attained political independence. His residence in Paris exacerbated his wandering, shattered subjectivity. Caught between two seemingly distinct worlds, societies, civilizations, etc., Idrīs was bound to undergo some kind of identity crisis, which would heavily affect his sense of self and what place he occupies within his Moroccan society, one he sees as lagging behind France/Europe.

It is important to highlight the fact that Laroui (b. 1933-) is a preeminent intellectual in Morocco and the Arabic-speaking world and that his oeuvre includes, in addition to fiction, significant critical volumes, such as the seminal *Al-'Idyūlūjyā al-'arabiyyah al-mu'āṣirah* (1967, Contemporary Arab Ideology) and *The Crisis of the Arab Intellectual: Traditionalism or Historicism?* (1974). Laroui has indeed been on "the vanguard in his treatment of questions of historiography, sociology, culture, politics, and the arts in relation to the Arabic-speaking world as it deals with the challenges of modernity"; for he attributes "this general predicament to Arabs' complicated relationship with *al-turāth* (heritage)" in the sense that Arabs are yet to fully comprehend and critique their past and heritage and, consequently, "remain deprived of the requisite tools to erect a real renaissance (*nahḍah*)" (El Younssi, 191—192). This lingering sense of failure casts its shadow on the entire novel *'Awrāq* and impacts the (shattered) subjectivity of its protagonist, Idrīs.

The title and subtitle of Laroui's novel (*Papers: Idrīs's Mental Biography*) *mirror* the structure of the text as a whole. The book, thus, consists of two fundamental substructures: First, the various writings of Idrīs and, second, the commentaries on this archive by the Narrator and Shu'ayb. One could, therefore, speak of at least two prominent narrative levels—as well as two narrative timeframes—in the text, with one pertaining to Idrīs's archive and the other to the perpetual discussions between the Narrator and Shuʿayb vis-à-vis this archive. This kind of structuring is foreshadowed in the title, and the subtitle shows how significant and deeply engrained the *mise en abîme* technique is in the different narrative layers of the text. Here, I would like to propose that *mirroring*—with the reduplication of images that it entails—constitutes the most remarkable, if not the defining, feature of the book's experimental impulse. Mirroring derives its significance from the fact that it becomes a mechanism for and a figure of both the loss of *subjectivity* and the recuperation of a new one. Accordingly, *mise en abîme* serves the double role of eradicating and building. It brings the *wandering* nature of Idrīs's subjectivity into sharp focus.

Aiding the reader and the critic to demystify some of the book's ambiguities, Laroui offers some significant cues. He has, for instance, alluded in the introduction to ʾAwrāq that *mise en abîme* constitutes a vital device in the book's narrative play:

قول الراوي قول من؟ قول شعيب قول من؟ ايهما قول المؤلف؟

للقارئ ان يفصل. له الحق ان يختزل الكِتاب في أوراق ادريس فقط ويستقل بالكلمة دون الراوي وشعيب [. . .] له الحق أن يرفض التمييز بين مؤلف كتاب "أوراق" وادريس كاتب أوراق والراوي جامعها ومرتبها وشعيب المعلق عليها وصاحب الكلمة الأخيرة في تأويلها.

إذا قرر أن يحكم على الجميع حكما واحدا فلاضير ان أجاب على السؤال التالي: ما غرض المؤلف من هذه التعددية، من "انعكاس الصورة في مرايا متقابلة" [. . .].

Whose say is the Narrator? Whose say is Shuʿayb's? Which of the two is the Author's?

It is up to the reader to judge. He has the right to reduce the book to Idrīs' papers only, and to have a say independently of the Narrator and Shuʿayb. [. . .] He has the right to reject the distinction between the author of the book ʾAwrāq and Idrīs (who wrote these papers) and the Narrator (who collected and organized them) and Shuʿayb (who commented on them.) If [the reader] decided to cast one judgment on them all, it would be fitting to raise this question: What is the Author's goal behind this multiplicity, this *mise en abîme* [. . .]? (Laroui, ʾAwrāq 7)

Laroui seems to suggest that the three main characters—Idrīs, Shuʿayb, and the Narrator—could be interpreted as mirroring one another and ultimately forming one single personality, which in turn mirrors the person Abdallah Laroui, the real author. This point finds some corroboration in ʾAwrāq, for there are a few instances where we notice an overlap between the identities of the three characters and Laroui. In the novel's preliminary section, curiously entitled "The Ghost of Shuʿayb" (*shabaḥ Shuʿayb*), we have the first round of discussions and debates between Shuʿayb and the Narrator, in which we learn that the Narrator is, in fact, an experienced writer. Addressing the Narrator, Shuʿayb says:

هذه أوراق إدريس، خذها، أنت أقرب الناس إليه [. . .]. الكتابة حرفتك. إفعل بها ما تراه نافعا.

These are Idrīs's papers. Take them. You are the closest to him. [. . .] Writing is your profession. Do with them [i.e., the papers] what you see fit. (9)

The Narrator initially displays some hesitation towards Shuʿayb's request that a biography of Idrīs be reconstructed based on the stack of papers Idrīs has left behind. He remarks that the papers are not in order and that they incorporate diverse styles, adding that if he were to arrange them as he wishes, he could give them meaning different from the one intended by Idrīs himself (9). And then he makes this revealing statement:

وإذا نشرت كل ما فيها على حاله ربما ألحقت به الضرر. قد أعطي عنه صورة أقل وفاء من تلك التي خططتها عندما جعلت منه شخصية خيالية.

If I were to publish [the papers] as they are, I could probably do him harm. I might give an image of him as less faithful than the one I put together when I made him an imaginary character. (9)

Being unsubstantiated, this statement leaves the reader and the critic somewhat perplexed and prone to make the provisional conclusion that the Narrator— who is putatively a writer by profession—has already begun composing a fictional piece centred around an imaginary character named after and inspired by Idr s, the late friend of the Narrator. Shu ayb also seems confounded by this revelation; he retorts:

استعملت اسمه وأقواله وحوادث حياته بدون إذن منه. الآن حان الوقت أن تؤدي له حقوقه.

You used his name, his sayings, and his life incidents without his permission. Now is the time to pay him back his dues. (9)

Shuʿayb is implying that the Narrator should take on the task of arranging Idrīs's papers and turning them into a biography. Before agreeing to honour this request, the Narrator points out that he is "convinced that the biography is an elusive concept" (9), given that "the individual is constant creation and constant fragmentation" (10). In other words, capturing a person's true self is an ever-slippery endeavour because of the perpetual change one's self goes through. (This comment could be read both literarily and philosophically.) The Narrator then proceeds to disclose more details about his past relationship with Idrīs as well as his fictional project involving Idrīs. He mentions that they both hail from the same village and neighbourhood and were companions at school, adding that he used to see Idrīs as "a mirror reflecting my soul and I a mirror reflecting his" (11). Then underscores that he made Idrīs a protagonist in a story he composed, where it is difficult to disentangle the thoughts, opinions, and beliefs of the two individuals (12). However, the Narrator tells us that, once he has leafed through Idrīs's stack of papers, he discovered a completely different person—which has left him wondering which of the two versions is "closer to reality" (12).

These revelations are indeed fascinating; they are pregnant with hints and allusions as to the (supposed) identity of the two characters (the Narrator and Idrīs) and the nature of the narrative game at work in the book. The *mise en abîme* motif is quite powerful in the metaphor of the mirror, which makes the two unite not just at the level of the soul but also at that of the body. We are told that the Narrator used to see his soul reflected in Idrīs's and that Idrīs, in turn, used to see his soul mirrored in the Narrator's. This serves the thesis of sameness at the spiritual and intellectual levels. (Let us remember that the Narrator says that Idrīs's *intellect* was his companion, which entails that the two share the same faculty of thinking and the same thought processes.) The corporeal level then comes in, albeit in the fictional realm, to complement the other two levels, the spiritual and the intellectual; the Narrator asserts that several people have held the belief that Idrīs, the character in the Narrator's fictional writing, was indeed an image of him, his look-alike or double.

It is important to underscore that we are led to this conclusion—of the Narrator and Idrīs being the same person—only through a two-dimensional inquiry that weaves together two narrative times and discourses: Firstly, the time of the uttering of the above quote, which presupposes the physical presence of Shuʿayb as the Narrator's interlocutor and, secondly, the time of the fictional piece the Narrator is supposedly composing about the half-imaginary, half-real character Idrīs. It is justifiable to follow this line of inquiry that aims at synthesizing the various pieces regarding Idrīs's fragmented, scattered self/subjectivity. This is in line with the very procedure of the Narrator and the literary vision of Laroui himself, a vision that sees value in mixing, doubling, multiplying, and overlapping, a vision that casts light on the *wandering* subjectivity of the Moroccan intellectual in the vicissitudes of postcoloniality. There is an echo here of that literary-philosophical motto of the Narrator, that the force of "creation" and "fragmentation" is ever at play (10). As one thing begets another, its identity as a unitary entity is, by default, impacted. The quote cited above (*Awrāq*, 11-12) alludes to the fiction within the fiction, to one story begetting another, thereby highlighting the forces of creation and fragmentation at work. The Narrator dissects the personality of his late friend

Idrīs, rendering him "the hero of a story." To *create* a story (something new) revolving around Idrīs, the Narrator cannot do without *dissecting* his person into bits and fragments. Put differently, for *construction* to take place, *deconstruction* becomes a necessity. In this context, deconstruction and *mise en abîme* are ultimately the same process. This idea symbolically aligns with the thesis of breaking a fixed subject(ivity) as a first step before forging a new one. It highlights how Laroui's experimental literary work serves his broader project of interrogating contemporary Moroccan and Arab ideologies. The Moroccan author is calling for a fundamental restructuring of Arab literary expression so that Arab societies can be reconciled with modernity in a meaningful and fruitful way. Such an act of restructuring would facilitate a reconstruction of Arab subjectivity, thus paving the way for true creativity on various fronts, including the literary craft. Laroui seeks to demonstrate that the realist novel—a vestige of European colonialism and a tool of its cultural imperialism—remains unsuitable for the Arab writer. Laroui is urging Arab writers to pursue other literary forms or configurations that would convincingly reflect and convey the socio-political exigencies of the Arab peoples in the postcolonial era.

As the conversation between Shuʿayb and the Narrator moves along, *mise en abîme* gains in prominence, and the reader finds additional clues about the hazy, unstable, and constantly shifting identity and subjectivity of the characters navigating the multiple narrative layers of the book. There is an additional key piece of information in the following quote uttered by the Narrator:

لا أسأل: من كفّن ودفن إدريس؟ أقول إنه مات ميتة أستاذه وأستاذي الذي اقتبست منه بعض ملامح شخصية يوليوس [. . .].

I am not asking: Who wrapped and buried Idrīs's body? I am saying that his death is *similar* to that of his teacher and my teacher, from whom I *borrowed* some of the features of *the character Julius*. (ʾ*Awrāq* 10; emphasis added)

A set of questions arises: Who is Julius? What do we know about him besides the fact that he was the teacher of both Idrīs and the Narrator? What role, if any, does he play in ʾ*Awrāq*? Fortunately for the reader, the quote above is accompanied by an endnote,[2] in which we learn that Julius is one of the

---

2 It is remarkable that Laroui provides endnotes to his book, a practice that is quite unorthodox in fictional writing. These endnotes amount to 139 in total. Commenting on this practice, Laroui explains: "The references that I included in ʾ*Awrāq* were meant to make things easier [for the reader], and they are justified [. . .]. [ʾ*Awrāq*] is a critical book or a critical study on a text. . . Thus, each one of these two people (the Narrator/Author and Shuʿayb) would try to show to the other the source of what he finds in the text. [. . .]

characters in Laroui's novel *Al-Ghurbah*³ and that he is based on a real person named François Gottland, who served as "a teacher of French Literature in Moulay Youssef High School" during French colonial presence in Morocco (*'Awrāq* 245). The autobiographical overtones of this endnote are noteworthy. Putting the Narrator's words in line with the information provided in the endnote, one is drawn to conclude that the Narrator is indeed the author of the novel *Al-Ghurbah*, meaning that he and Laroui constitute the same person. This is further corroborated by the fact that the main character in *Al-Ghurbah* is no other than Idrīs.

With that said, Julius emerges as another double of Idrīs, at least at the technical, "meta-fictional" level; just as the Narrator borrowed some of the characteristics of his "imaginary" character Idrīs from the "real" person Idrīs, he borrowed some of the features of the character Julius from the real person François Gottland. This trope of mirroring and reduplication is maintained through the flow of the Narrator's revelations. Although he does not imply that Idrīs and Julius are completely identical, the Narrator alludes to some similarities between the two and how their respective destinies seem to mirror one another. The Narrator wonders if Julius died of depression due to France's failure or perhaps due to his own professional, political, or emotional failure, adding that he must have left "some *papers*, and that some people intend to make them public to answer the question: Why? Why?" (11) It is telling that the questions the Narrator raises about the death of Julius are similar to and parallel the questions he and Shu'ayb are asking regarding Idrīs's death. The juxtaposition of Idrīs's and Julius's destinies highlights an important period of Morocco's modern history: colonial time. Laroui draws on the French colonial enterprise in the country to illuminate and give more context to Idrīs's existential and intellectual journeys and to pinpoint its impact on his troubled, wandering subjectivity.

It appears as though the most important reason why Shu'ayb and the Narrator are discussing and debating the papers left behind by Idrīs is to figure out what caused his premature death at forty. On the first page of the section entitled "The Ghost of Shu'ayb," we learn that Idrīs lived "twenty years in the darkness of [French] colonialism and twenty years in the light of [Morocco's] independence" (9), which helps the reader determine the exact historical period that Idrīs lived: 1936-1976. In the section following the last chapter of

---

The way in which this text—which is a text on a text—was written justifies this procedure [. . .]." See Muḥammad Al-Dāhī, *Shi'riyyat al-sīrah al-dhihniyyah* (The Poetics of the Intellectual (Auto)Biography) (Cairo: Ru'yah, 2008), 160.

³ This was Laroui's first literary work, and it was published in 1971.

'*Awrāq*—which takes the title *Al-Ta'bīn* or "Commemoration" (234—42)—the Narrator and Shuʿayb engage in a heated debate over what exactly caused or led to Idrīs's demise. The Narrator notes that because he did not have access to what Idrīs wrote about himself he was under the impression that "Māriyyah's infidelity" was the cause of his affliction; he adds that after having "read and arranged his papers [he] can see that [Idrīs] only saw himself in the context of failure and disappointment" and that he "decided that his failure would be the true expression of the collective failure" (234). The Narrator, perhaps unsurprisingly, maintains the game of mixing and overlapping different narrative layers and narrative times in this passage. He splits Idrīs into two, the "imaginary Idrīs"— who take the role of protagonist in the novel *Al-Ghurbah*—and the "real Idrīs"— who wrote the papers under investigation in the novel '*Awrāq*. This rhetorical move is by no means made explicit in the quote but is a logical conclusion to critics and readers familiar with Laroui's previous literary works—namely the following novels: *Al-Ghurbah*, *Al-Yatīm* (The Orphan), and *Al-Farīq* (The Team). The passage mentions in passing Māriyyah, who is a major character in Laroui's first novel, *Al-Ghurbah*—a work that is also claimed by the Narrator, as we have seen earlier—and the second novel, *Al-Yatīm*. The Narrator makes a comparison between the two images of Idrīs, the one originating in *Al-Ghurbah* and the other springing from the papers, which '*Awrāq* treats as true historical documents. As the Narrator would have us believe, the literary (i.e., the fictional Idrīs of *Al-Ghurbah*) is adjacent to, interacts with, and feeds off the extra-literary (i.e., the real Idrīs). It is curious—and remains unaccounted for—why the Narrator would mix up these two levels in the quest for what precipitated the death of the "historical" Idrīs.

Nonetheless, the idea of "failure" occupies a prominent position in the Narrator's assessment of the papers and is taken as a critical factor behind the death of the "historical" Idrīs. This notion of "failure" brings to light not only Idrīs's internal struggles with literary writing but also gives the reader a sense of Idrīs's outside world, highlighting thereby the dialectic of the private and the public. Idrīs sees himself as an extension, maybe the embodiment, of his society's failures—which interestingly connects to a fundamental thesis of Laroui's, namely the state of crisis and "loss of the subject" assailing Moroccan and Arab societies in the twentieth century—and perhaps beyond. In his critical work *Al-ʾIdyūlūjyā al-ʿarabiyyah al-muʿāṣirah* (Contemporary Arab Ideology), Laroui writes:

قد يكون موضوعنا هو بالضبط ضياع الموضوع، لكن في ظروف خاصة بنا، ولا يكون إبداع بدون تخصيص. وقد يكون شأنا آخر أكثر إيجابية. كل الأبواب إذن أمامنا، لكن لا تنفتح أية واحدة منها إلا لمن سلك طريق النقد الصارم. [. . .]

والبحث عن الموضوع أليس وجهاً من البحث عن الذات، محور هذا الكتاب؟

Our subject could exactly be *loss of the subject*, albeit in circumstances peculiar to us [Arabs]—and there is no creativity without specificity. And it could be another thing, a more positive one. All doors, therefore, are before us, but none would open unless we pursued *rigorous criticism*. [. . .]

And isn't the search for the subject another facet of the search for the *self*, the core issue of this book? (*Al-ʾIdyūlūjyā* 22; emphasis added)

This key notion of "loss of the subject," which connotes Arabs' loss of their subjectivity and identity, undergirds the entirety of the novel *ʾAwrāq* and informs the myriad discussions and debates between Shuʿayb and the Narrator over Idrīs' stack of papers. The Narrator continues his concluding remarks on the late Idrīs as follows:

[. .] حكم على نفسه باليأس القاتل. لم يكن في مستوى طموحه كما لم يكن مجتمعه في مستوى آماله. مات كما مات غيره من العجز والحسرة. [. . .] والآن جاء الوقت لأقول كلمتي الأخيرة: الكتابة انسلاخ وانتحار، استجابة لإخفاق الحياة الجماعية.

[. . .] He condemned himself to fatal disappointment. He did not live up to what he had aspired to, and *his society* did not meet his hopes. He died of impotence and agony, just like the other(s). [. . .] And now comes the time for me to say my final word:

Writing is detachment and suicide, a response to the *failure* of the life of the *collective*. (*ʾAwrāq*, 236—38; emphasis added)

This passage can be read as painting a triangular relationship involving three interconnected entities: Idrīs, his society, and literary writing. Idrīs has indeed struggled tremendously while attempting to become a writer. As we are made to understand, he ultimately fails in this task for a panoply of reasons, including, for one, his society's condition (i.e., the contextual or extra-literary) and, secondly, the encroachment of the social—what Laroui calls "*al-mawṣūf*" (literally, the described)—on his literary writing (i.e., the textual or literary). According to Laroui, *al-mawṣūf* is the antithesis of the concept of *al-mawḍūʿ* ("the subject") as far as literary writing goes. After glossing over European forms, such as the novel and the short story, Laroui asserts:

إن الموضوع ليس هو الموصوف. لكي يصبح الموصوف موضوعا لابد من تحوير وتطويع الأشكال السردية حتى تصبح قادرة على عكس أغراضنا في البنى نفسها. [. . .]

The subject is not "the described." In order for "the described" to become a subject, narrative forms must be imploded and mastered until they become capable of reflecting our [Moroccan/Arab] exigencies in *the structures themselves*. [. . .] (*Al-ʾIdyūlūjyā*, 21—22)

Literary form, thus, becomes a central arena reflecting and enfolding Arab socio-political exigencies. In other words, literary writing becomes a key site for reconstructing the disjointed elements of Arab/Moroccan subjectivity and identity. It is, hence, indispensable for both the protagonist Idrīs's and the Arab collective's attempts to recuperate *al-mawdū* ("the subject").

The private-public dialectic, as it connects to the notion of "failure", shows another dimension of the *mirroring* technique running through *'Awrāq*, namely in bringing together the destinies of Idrīs and his former teacher Julius. As we have seen above, the Narrator wonders if Julius' death was caused by his professional, political, or emotional failures. These three types of failure also sum up what could have precipitated Idrīs's demise. At the *professional* level, Idrīs failed to fulfil his dream of turning into a successful writer despite his constant efforts and the many concrete steps he has taken to reach that goal. In one of his papers, Idrīs writes that since he was a child, he always "dreamed of becoming a writer" despite the fact that his family pressured him to study medicine (*'Awrāq* 90). Idrīs passionately wanted writing to be his primary profession, not just a hobby. He could not imagine himself being anything other than a writer. That is why he went against his family's wishes and took the bold step of "enrolling himself in the department of letters" (41). We also learn that he "refused to take teaching as a profession" (41). Commenting on Idrīs's "rebellion" against his family, the Narrator notes that this behaviour perhaps shows the extent to which he was influenced by "the enemies of [the institution of] the family (Nietzsche, Gide, and Sartre)" (91). Interestingly, in the discussion between Shu'ayb and the Narrator regarding Idrīs's paper, in which our protagonist reflects on his family's pressuring him to opt for medicine and his final decision to join "the department of letters" instead, we get a few hints on how Idrīs's career choice has a *political* dimension. In fact, this particular piece of paper consists of two paragraphs, with the first treating his professional career and the second disclosing his political sensibility. It is revealing that Idrīs concludes this piece on a political note. Reacting to the misery of a young boy selling meat sandwiches on the street, he says: "This is what France has done to us" (91). The Narrator and Shu'ayb take up this reference, providing the reader with more context. On his part, the Narrator states that Idrīs constructed this piece of writing while residing at the university dorm "Morocco House" in Paris and "hearing and reading a lot on the Moroccan crisis" (91). We learn afterwards that this refers to the August 20, 1953 crisis (93) when the French colonial authorities forced then King Mohamed V of Morocco into exile in Corsica and then Madagascar.[4]

The Narrator is forthcoming in showing the contradictions in Idrīs's personality, especially with respect to the private-public dialectic. He remarks that after Idrīs has abandoned his own small family and then set himself free from being attached to his former teacher Julius, he returned to "the bosom of a larger family in the heart of Paris"; he adds that Idrīs tossed "Gide's teachings [. . .], and instead of screaming, 'I despise you, o family,' he says 'I hate you, o France'" (Laroui, *'Awrāq*, 92). The larger family here refers to the Moroccan nation and speaks to Idrīs's growing nationalist feelings. He could not liberate himself from his external attachments, which would negatively impact his literary ambitions and would ultimately lead to his professional downfall, his supposed failure as a writer (237). Here, we see how intricately related the professional and political dimensions of Idrīs's life journey are. It is noteworthy that the quote above alludes to the character of Julius, who is also taken as being part of the external world that tightened its grip on Idrīs's soul and intellect. The parallels between Idrīs and his former teacher, Julius, at the professional and political levels did not prevent the two from standing on opposite sides of the political spectrum. Julius is a supporter of French colonial presence in Morocco, and he takes part (and probably pride) in the *mission civilisatrice* by becoming a colonial settler and taking a high school teaching position on Moroccan soil. His nationalism mirrors that of Idrīs. This brings to mind an earlier quote, in which the Narrator muses on whether Julius's death was caused by "France's failure" about the Nazis' occupation of French territories during World War II. Just as Julius could not stand seeing his homeland becoming a German colony, Idr s was irritated—probably devastated—by Morocco being a French colony/protectorate. The mirroring motif reaches its height when the Narrator notes that Julius has probably, just like Idrīs, left several papers and that some of his kin might be considering their publication.

The Narrator's musing on a possible emotional cause behind Julius' passing could be seen as mirroring Idrīs's emotional failure, namely the devastating effect of the infidelity of the woman he deeply loved, Māriyyah—an aspect of Idrīs's life journey that is treated at length in Laroui's previous novels *al-Ghurbah* and *al-Yatīm*. I should add that Idrīs's other love misfortunes do make an appearance in *'Awrāq*. In chapter seven, aptly titled "Emotion," we come to learn of how Idrīs while living in Paris, met a German girl and how their

---

[4] See, for example, Egya N. Sangmuah, "Sultan Mohammed ben Youssef's American Strategy and the Diplomacy of North African Liberation, 1943-61," *Journal of Contemporary History* 27.1 (1992): 129-148, 139.

relationship ended after only a few weeks (149). The Narrator comments that Idrīs's behaviour with the German girl shows that "his emotional education" was not on par with "his intellectual education" (149). After they parted ways, Idrīs continued to draft letters to the German girl for an entire year, although the reader is not sure if he (Idrīs) took the step of mailing any of them. As we come to learn afterwards, "Idrīs lived with the ghost of the German girl throughout the year of 1957 until he met another girl, a Frenchwoman this time, whom [he] also treated like a ghost" as their relationship once again ended in failure (161). This period in Idrīs's life coincided with the time when he was deeply immersed in reading Marcel Proust, from whom he learned that literary writing is "deception" (166). Proust seems to have penetrated the ghostly love life of Idrīs by infiltrating the letters he has written for both the German and the French girls. When drafting those letters, "Idrīs was addressing himself" (165) and at the same time experimenting with (literary) writing. Commenting on this interesting detail, the Narrator notes the letter, as a medium, was from the start a way for Idrīs "to invoke himself," adding that in "the final phase of the progression [...] the letter dissolved into pure *literary* description," which meant that Idrīs could now "write directly, i.e., addressing the unknown reader" (165). This shows the extent to which Idrīs's love fiascos affected his adventures with literary writing. The letter served as a linchpin, bringing his emotions to bear on the literary wor(l)ds he was constructing or, rather, wished to construct.

It becomes clear that the notion of failure—professional, political, emotional or otherwise—figures as a significant trope linking the characters of Idrīs and Julius. More importantly, it serves as a reminder of how deeply ingrained *mise en abîme* is in the book *ʾAwrāq*. Fittingly, *mise en abîme* also runs through some of the pieces Idrīs has himself drafted. In the early excerpts from Idrīs's semi-autobiographical writings that we encounter in chapter one (cf. pages 15-19), we see that he has taken the character of *al-fatā* (the young man) as a protagonist. Here is one example:

ودّع الفتى مرافقيه على رأس الدرب وتابع طريقه نحو باب المنزل العائلي الذي كان يبعد بعشرة أمتار عن الطريق الذاهب إلى البيضاء.

The young man said good goodbye to his friends at the end of the alley and continued his way towards the family house that was ten meters away from the road to Casablanca. (15)

This passage is part of Idrīs's very first attempts with writing, and it dates back to the time when his family sent him to a boarding school far away from his hometown; we would later learn that the school is in the city of Rabat (28). It is noteworthy that Idr s, although still a teenager, demonstrates a precocious literary sensibility, for instead of writing about himself in a direct fashion in the first person, he has opted for creating a pseudo-imaginary character with the nomenclature of "*al-fatā*," experimenting thereby with the technique of *mise en abîme*. This could be the first sign of his journey towards creative writing, towards fulfilling the dream of becoming a successful writer. In his capacity as commentator and critic, the Narrator exposes Idrīs's employment of *mise en abîme*; he affirms that "from the start Idrīs lived on two levels," adding that "he dissolved in the character of *al-fatā*" so that he could "contemplate its features and inspect its conduct" clearly (16). After examining more passages in which Idrīs strives to depict *literarily* the character of *al-fatā*, the Narrator makes an assessment of utmost importance; he tells Shuʿayb:

ألاحظ بالفعل خللا في التركيب ناتجا عن استهداف الموضوعية. أراد إدريس أن ينفصل عن نفسه ليتأملها منعكسة في مرآة. فخطط لحياة مخالفة لحياته. غير أنه لم يصمد أمام هجمة الواقع. إنهار السد الواقي وتكسرت المرآة. [. . .] واضح أن إدريس حاول أن ينزع الخصوصية عن المناظر التي أحاطت بشبابنا. إلا أن المحاولة لم تكلل بالنجاح. اخترق الواقع حائط الخيال [. . .].

I notice a *flaw* in the composition resulting from targeting objectivity. Idrīs wanted to be separated from himself so that he could see it reflected in a *mirror*. And so he planned for a life different from his, only he could not withstand the attack of *reality*. The protective barricade dissolved, and the *mirror* broke. [. . .] Clearly, Idrīs tried to remove specificity from the scenes surrounding our youth, but he did not find success. Reality penetrated the wall of the imagination. (19—20, emphasis added)

Following the Narrator, Idrīs could not handle well the *mise en abîme* technique, and therefore, his attempts to craft a literary piece that gives priority to the imagination to the detriment of reality/realism did not find success. He could not maintain a good and convincing distance between the two levels of his wandering self. The mirror metaphor went to pieces, and the literary effect of mirroring followed suit. Idrīs's imaginative faculty faces limits with the encroachment of reality on his literary realms. He could not rid himself of the heavy toll of the mundane details of everyday life. In short, he finds himself unable to go past *al-mawṣūf* (the described), and thus his goal of grasping *al-mawdūʿ* (the subject) and transcribing it in his writing remains unreachable, hence the lingering sense of loss and crisis that marks the book *ʾAwrāq*, reflective of Idrīs's wandering, shattered subjectivity. Idrīs thus turns into a trope embodying and mirroring the colossal crises that assailed Arab societies and nation-states in the last century, both during and after the European colonial enterprise.

Works Cited

Al-Dāhī, Muḥammad. *Shi'riyyat al-sīrah al-dhihniyyah* (The Poetics of the Intellectual (Auto)Biography). Cairo: Ru'yah, 2008.

El Younssi, Anouar. "'Abdullāh al-'Arwī's *'Awrāq: sīrat Idrīs al-dhihniyyah* and the Aesthetics-Politics Dialectic." *Journal of Arabic Literature* 54, 1-2 (2023): 189-216.

Laroui, Abdallah. *Al-Farīq* (The Team). Casablanca: al-Markaz al-Thaqāfī al-'Arabī, 2001, 1986.

---. *Al-Ghurbah* (Estrangement). Casablanca: al-Markaz al-Thaqāfī al-'Arabī, 2000, 1971.

---. *Al-'Idyūlūjyā al-'arabiyyah al-mu'āṣirah* (Contemporary Arab Ideology). Casablanca: Al-Markaz Al-Thaqāfī Al-'Arabī, 1995, 1970.

---. *Al-Yatīm* (The Orphan). Casablanca: al-Markaz al-Thaqāfī al-'Arabī, 2001, 1978.

---. *'Awrāq: sīrat Idrīs al-dhihniyyah* (Papers: Idrīs's Intellectual Biography). Casablanca: Al-Markaz Al-Thaqāfī Al-'Arabī, 1996, 1989.

---. *Les carnets d'Idris.* Casablanca: Centre Culturel Arabe, 2007.

---. *The Crisis of the Arab Intellectual: Traditionalism or Historicism?* Berkeley: University of California Press, 1976.

Sangmuah, Egya. "Sultan Mohammed ben Youssef's American Strategy and the Diplomacy of North African Liberation, 1943-61." *Journal of Contemporary History* 27.1 (1992): 129-148.

Acknowledgements

This book would not have been conceived if it were not for the paper presentation at the African Literature Association Conference (2022), and for Julien Verdeaux from Vernon Press who recognized its potential for the paper to expand to a book. Much appreciation is due to the conveners of the conference, to my fellow panel members and to the publishers. The discussion that ensued from the presentation on that day plays a pivotal role in the formation of the book, with the title itself borrowed from the panel title. Thanks to Anu Kuriakose for readily agreeing to work on this book project and help compile it in the present form. My indebtedness also to my PhD supervisor, S Sharmila, as this book is an extension to the thoughts garnered into my PhD thesis with her prompts and provocation.

As editors, we are grateful to the anonymous reviewers who agreed to peer review the chapters and to the scholars who shared encouraging words after reviewing the book. Thanks to Anirban Bose for lending his creativity for the book cover. Our thanks to the contributors, without whom the book would be non-existent, is immense.

Contributors

Namrata Nirmal: Namrata Nirmal is an External Consultant with the Word Lab at the Indian Institute for Human Settlements (IIHS). She provides editorial support for book publications, academic writing, and grey literature. She is an associate editor of *Urbanisation*, IIHS's biannual journal published by Sage Publications. Namrata holds an integrated Master's in English Studies, with a minor in Development Studies, from IIT Madras, where she researched the literary representation of women in the city with a focus on Indian English fiction.

Merin Simi Raj: Merin Simi Raj is an Associate Professor (English) in the Department of Humanities and Social Sciences at IIT Madras. She is the faculty coordinator of the Centre for Memory Studies and the co-founder and chairperson of the Indian Network for Memory Studies (INMS), the first national network in Asia under the aegis of the International Memory Studies Association (MSA). She researches in memory studies, historiography and modernity studies, Anglo-Indian studies, and digital humanities. She co-edited the volume *Anglo-Indian Identities: Past and Present, in India and the Diaspora* (Palgrave Macmillan, 2021) and is currently co-editing the *Brill Indian Handbook for Memory Studies*.

Jintu Alias: Jintu Alias is an institute fellow (PhD) in the Department of Literature and Languages at SRM University, Andhra Pradesh, India. Her research revolves around the representation of Kochi and its cosmopolitanism in fiction. Some of her work has been published in *Cultural Geographies*, *Journal of Postcolonial Writing and Modern Jewish Studies*.

Aleena Achamma Paul: Aleena Achamma Paul is a Doctoral Scholar in English in the Department of Humanities and Social Sciences at IIT Ropar, India. Her research interests include contemporary American literature, science fiction, queer theory, and gender studies. Her essays have appeared in *Literature Compass*, among others. ORCID: https://orcid.org/0000-0003-1555-5511

Sakti Sekhar Dash: Sakti Sekhar Dash is a Fellow of the Social Science Research Council, Open Association of Research Society, USA. He holds a PhD from Ravenshaw University, India. With a profound interest in literature, history, and culture, he has extensively studied the myths, legends, and folklore of ancient Greece, Egypt, Rome, and India. As a researcher, he loves to revisit and re-examine ancient texts from multiple perspectives. An experienced educator and honorary member of the Illinois Medieval Association, he has served as the editor-in-chief of an international peer-reviewed journal. He has extensively written and published on a diverse range of topics, including modernism, Greek drama, environmental studies, Theatre of the Absurd, and Shakespearean drama.

Jabeen Yasmeen: Jabeen Yasmeen holds a PhD from the Indian Institute of Technology Bombay. Her dissertation was on narrating the Nellie Massacre of 1983. She is a recipient of the 2019 Zubaan-Sasakawa Peace Foundation Grants for Young Researchers from the Northeast. Her areas of interest are Trauma Narratives, Oral History, Storytelling, Partition Studies, Literature on identity and citizenship, and literature from Northeast India.

Ijeoma Odoh: Dr. Ijeoma D. Odoh has been a Lecturer at Princeton University, New Jersey, USA since September 2011. She has also been teaching part-time at Rutgers University, New Brunswick, since September 2022. She completed her doctoral program in English Studies at Howard University, Washington DC, in May 2018. Her dissertation explores post-war migration and 20th-21st Century Black British Women's Literature. Prior to joining Howard University, she was an Assistant Lecturer at the Directorate of General Studies, Federal University of Technology, Owerri Imo State, Nigeria. She was also a Research Associate at Five College Women's Studies Research Center, Mount Holyoke College South Hadley MA (2009-2010), and a Visiting Scholar at the African Studies Department, Michigan State University, East Lansing (2010-2011). Her research focuses on Postwar Migration and Diaspora Studies, Black British Women's Writing, Women's and Gender Studies, African Literature, Postcolonial Literature, and her theory on Rhizomatic Womb-Space.

Anindita Chatterjee: Dr Anindita Chatterjee is an Associate Professor and Head of the Department of English, Durgapur Government College, West Bengal. She did a PhD on "John Clare: Poetry of Madness" from Jadavpur University. She also completed two Minor Research Projects, one on Representation of 'modern' India in the Fictions of Chetan Bhagat (funded by UGC) and the other, "Sari Story: Dressing the Indian Woman through History, 'Tracing the Origin, Growth and Evolution of the Traditional Indian Wear" (funded by ICSSR). She has co-edited *Re- theorising the Indian Subcontinental Diaspora: Old and New Directions* (CSP: 2020) and *Covid-19 in India, Disease, Health and Culture* (Routledge: 2022). She has published a book chapter in *Indian Feminist Ecocriticism* (Lexington Books, 2022), *Modernist Transitions* (Bloomsbury, 2023), *Desertscapes in the Global South and Beyond: Anthropocene Naturecultures* (Routledge, 2023) and articles in *Textile- Cloth and Culture* (Taylor and Francis) and *Contemporary Review of the Middle East* (Sage). She has guest edited an Issue of *Café Dissensus* on '(Re)storying Indian Handloom Saree Culture' (Issue 68: April 2023). Her areas of interest include Nineteenth-Century British Literature, Gender Studies and Popular Culture. She is currently authoring a book on sari-sutra. ORCID: https://orcid.org/00 00-0003-1244-5544)

Anouar El Younssi: Dr Anouar El Younssi is an Assistant Professor of Arabic and Middle Eastern Studies at Oxford College of Emory University in the US. He holds a BA in English Literature and Linguistics, an MA in English, and a PhD in Comparative Literature. His scholarly work explores the wave of literary innovation in modern Arabic literatures, with a focus on Morocco and the Maghreb region.

Index

www.ingramcontent.com/pod-product-compliance
Lightning Source LLC
Chambersburg PA
CBHW050523280326
41932CB00014B/2428